I0755166

ISBN: 978-1-962935-83-8

First edition 2025.

Published by High Tide Publications - www.hightidepublications.com

Front Cover design by Kathleen P. Decker and Jeanne M. Johansen

Printed in the United States of America.

Editor's Note:

This anthology began as a joint project between myself, Dr. Laura Guertin, and Betsy Wilkening. Dr. Guertin and Betsy Wilkening have been creating fascinating exhibits at the American Geophysical Union Fall Meetings since 2021 which combine their love of fiber art with science. Their goal has been to educate, amuse, and inform the public about topics of scientific interest and to raise public awareness about global warming, climate change, threats to the environment, and other changes to our planet, as well as some possible solutions. The first year centered on fiber art quilt creations, and since 2022, entries have expanded to other forms of fiber art.

In 2024, I suggested that we create a multi-modal ekphrastic project in which we paired fiber art with poetry. A number of poems were created in time for the December, 2024 American Geophysical Union exhibit to pair with fiber art. Throughout 2024 and early 2025, we accepted more submissions to create this book. Thus, some of the artwork in this book that was added after the conference is in the form of drawings, paintings, and even art in museums. However, each artwork accepted for the book was carefully chosen to fit with the theme-to explore "making the unseen, seen" and to link science and art through poetry.

The reader is strongly encouraged to read the Artist/Scientist Statements at the back of the book. They are wonderfully illuminating and even non-scientists can learn from the brief explanations of the colorful illustrations that accompany the thoughtful poems on topics that concern us all.

It has been a joy and a deeply satisfying challenge to match these poems with artists to create this book. We hope the reader will peruse the pages multiple times to glean deeper meanings through the layers of its pages. I am grateful to have such distinguished Associate Editors and colleagues as Dr. Guertin and Betsy Wilkening. It is a continuing pleasure to work with Jeanne Johansen and High Tide Publications to create such fine publications as this book!

~Dr. Kathleen P. Decker, Editor-in-Chief

Associate Editors: Dr. Laura Guertin, Betsy Wilkening

Foreword

Making the Unseen Seen is a perfect title for this ekphrastic book. While the poems and images reveal and illustrate the intricacies of nature and our ecosystems and sometimes, our effect on them, the title is, of course, a metaphor. I am certainly no scientist or medical doctor. I am an artist and writer, and past president of The Poetry Society of Virginia. From my artistic viewpoint it is more natural for me to operate from an aesthetic perspective first and an intellectual perspective second. Still, the science is pervasive.

A quilt created by Dr. Kathleen P. Decker (President of the Poetry Society of Virginia) entitled "The Unseen Battle" required an intriguing bit of research and application. Decker printed electron micrographic photos of SARS-CoV-2 neutralizing antibodies onto fabric, then stitched using raw edge appliqué, and embellished with Angelina fiber and metallic thread. Green beads highlighted the active binding site to host protein Angiotensin Converting Enzyme 2 (ACE2). The result is a lovely, deceivingly beautiful combination of pastel, stitched, white and yellow pieces of fabric floating on a blue background like flower petals dispersing in the wind. Her paired poem, "The Unseen Battle," begins with straightforward verbiage that leads the reader into a hospital then to minute blood vessels and in following stanzas, back to full size like a Hollywood Dolly-zoom. *inside brick hospital walls/down long corridors/ behind sliding glass doors/behind an oxygen mask/deep within blood vessels/the unseen battle rages.*

It is amazing that the English language, with its roots in Greek and Latin, can, with scientific verbiage, create its own rhythms and patterns. With technical terms such as birefringence (double refraction), lacustrine, bifurcated, and algorithms, these poets create internal rhymes and unusual rhythms. For instance, *We could, of course,/ Count the components of love: cisternae,/ Lipids, translocons, amino acids, all aflow/* as Donald Beagle suggests. And in his final stanza, sums up, *Where blood is the only truth and in/ Twilight distance the Tallis choirs sing Latin/ Incantations rhyming with "reticulum."/.* Here the language is handled with not just precision, but care.

In "Ghost Guests" by Mattie Quesenberry Smith (our current Poet Laureate of Virginia), we see that *Right here on the ridge, we cannot till three inches/Of topsoil without tipping out dead ends of limestone,/Without uncovering fossilized remnants of time spent/ When water washed through the creatures of the earth/And covered House Mountain. They were: cephalopods,/Brachiopods, graptolites, and three-lobed trilobites./ Trilobites.* What a fun word to say. I love the "l," lightly touching my tongue to my lower teeth, like "trill," a word that echoes the ridges of their exoskeletons.

"Dynamic positioning" describes how a ship maintains its place using thrusters and propellers while coring. Laura Guertin simply and precisely explains the process in "Maintaining Ship Position At Sea." And what an apt metaphor for humans in the ecosystem is the term, dynamic position.

Other poems omit scientific terminology altogether and carry their meaning with strands of beautiful language. In "The Colors of Music" by Zoey Dudding, we see that "… music dances/…/silently/humming cerulean sentences,/settling/in numbness of their afterglow,/ inky ebony seeping/through seams of milkwhite lavender, frosted/with chalky, muted silence./

Some poems blend the poetic with the scientific, as with current Poetry Society of Virginia Northern Region VP Cathy Hailey's "H-A-B, poem of pi and half pi." */nutrient beads infusing bright green roving infiltrating calm conditions/a shawl of looming toxicity/* What a superb metaphor. The accompanying fabric art shawl by Michale Glennon is a crocheted, knitted and hand-stitched semi-circle with a bright, yellow sun in the center of the flat edge. The larger sections are woven throughout with mostly greens and grays. It does, indeed, look like algae beneath a bright sun.

And then there's humor, in the form of an art quilt entitled "Solar Eclipse Glasses" by Barbara M. Linde, a delightfully bright, yellow and gold circular quilt "wearing" the eclipse glasses with which most of us are familiar. Paired with the poem, "Eclipse Rays by Suntana," also by Linde, to be sung to the tune of "Evil Ways" by Carlos Santana, it's a piece that will bring a smile and nod of familiarity. *You've got to stop those solar rays, viewer/Before they start hurtin' you./ Protect your eyes, viewer./So do what NASA says you should do./*

This is one book that needs no eye protection—it's intellectual eye candy. Enjoy and learn.

Terry Cox-Joseph
April, 2025

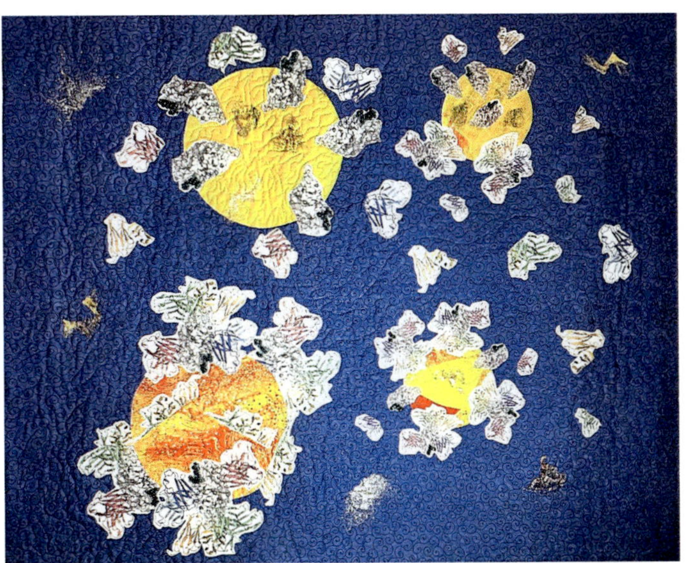

Art Quilt: "The Unseen Battle" by Kathleen P. Decker

Colour in a Polarised World*

Greg McNamara

We are such anisotropic beings
Our neuronic lattices bifurcate our inputs
Rays of thought fast and slow right and wrong
Yet so isotropic, at least in self-opinion,
such hubris
Rejecting our double refractions despite their logic
In favour of the certainty of total extinction
Wishing to be as solid as a garnet,
as opaque as a pyrite
living in willful ignorance of our birefringence.

*First published in *ConsilARTe,* v. 16, March, 2024

MAKING THE UNSEEN, **SEEN**

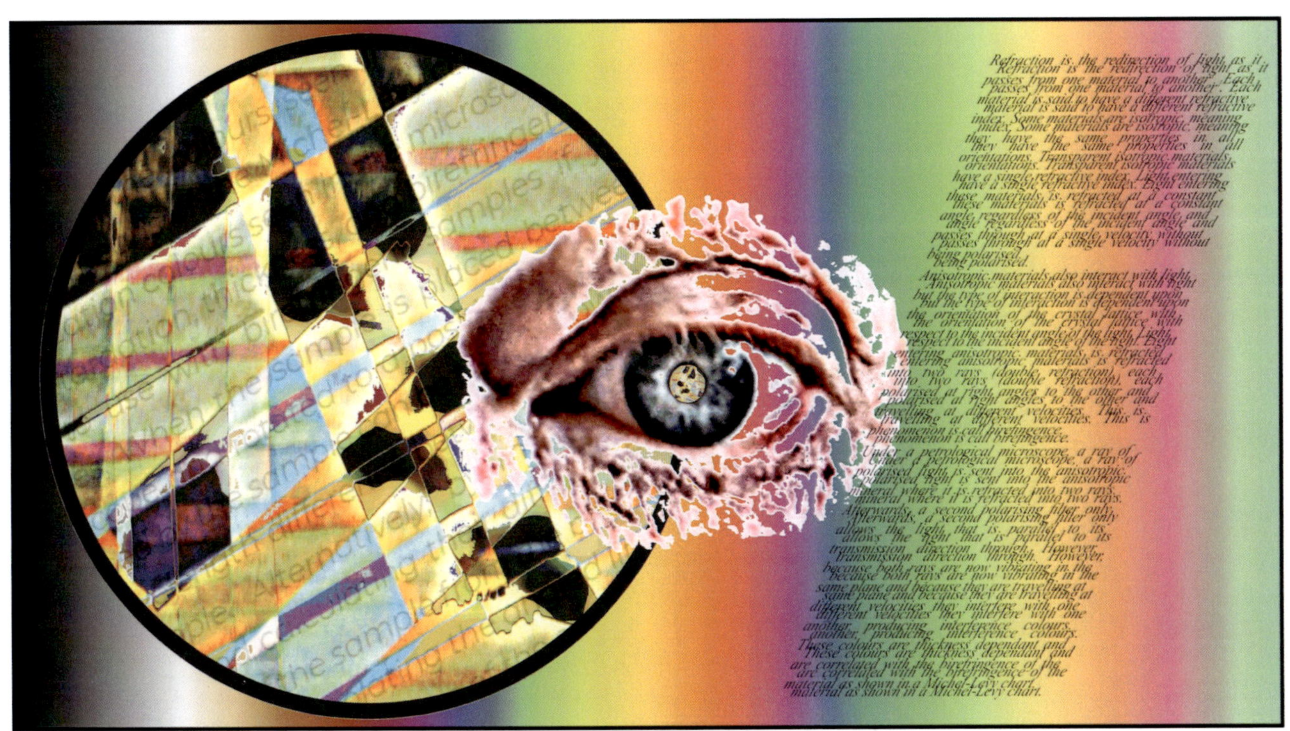

Graphic Art: "Colour in a Polarised World" by Greg McNamara*

TABLE OF CONTENTS: **PAGE(S)**

TABLE OF CONTENTS, cont'd.: **PAGE(S)**

TABLE OF CONTENTS, cont'd.: **PAGE(S)**

TABLE OF CONTENTS, cont'd.: **PAGES**

SECTION I: RARELY SEEN BEYOND EARTH

PSO J318.5-22

Dennis Owen Frohlich

deep within the galaxy
abandoned by its mother star
a planet free from gravity
lonely, empty, wandering far

flung into the black of space
unmoored from orbits constricting
receiving only light's faint trace
melancholy maledicting

then a comet flashes bright!
burning icy blue and white
offering momentary delight
then gone into the abyss

millennia pass, a light emerges
from the cosmic backdrop wide
toward a star the planet surges
gravity as guide

but now it's moving much too fast!
the planet slingshots quickly past
watching dreams recede, aghast
back into the endless dark

Gravity: It Must Be Good for Something

R. J. Keeler

Your concentric spheres hum;
        like an oiled bank-vault tumbler,
they click right into place.
But our gravitational attraction,
        so action-at-a-distance,
so Newtonian, so passé—
        drag us away, please, from that so-sheltered era.

I have been torn enough apart
        by transitioning through your event horizons.
So, go wave your silky multi-colorful scarfs—
        then mmmm!—make our joint spacetimes ripple and twist.

Your weak interactions tickle my under-quarks.
All around me my sparse tensors prickle.
Slow, like a lone insect sliding down into a tropical pitcher-plant,
        I glide down your spinning
                torqued-up, neutron-star body.

We dance there.
Gravitonic waves lash us together.
We renormalize.
We interchange our hottest photons.
We settle down to dote on each other.

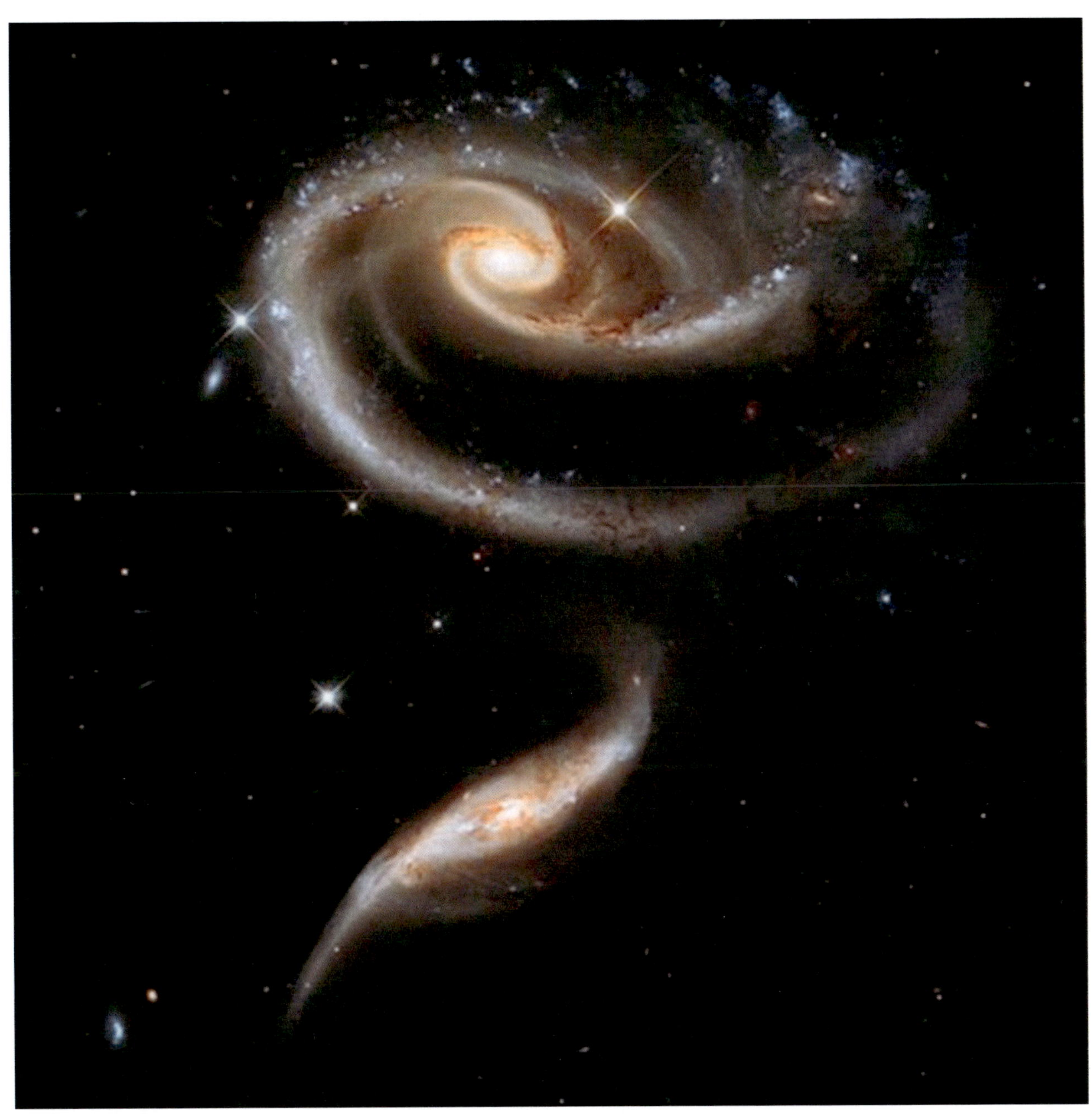

Image Credit: NASA

Dark Glasses
Suzanne Underwood Rhodes

The morning of the day the sun took flight,
I lean my arms on the fence to watch the cows
in their green kingdom grazing,
the grass lit with spring, everything hopeful.

I greet them, the patient mothers with heavy teats,
the new calves feeding, the moon's wheel
turning slowly sunward unbeknownst I think
to them in their simple pleasures.

I am different in my knowing. I know
from fact what's coming: time inching
toward the dark, the dark canceling the sun,
know to remove my glasses to glimpse the unseen,

then put them back on lest I go blind.
The cows know what cows know,
a few minutes of darker grass at noon.
Their lives happen only in time,
ours in the unknown.

This poem first appeared in Cave Region Review, issue 15, 2025

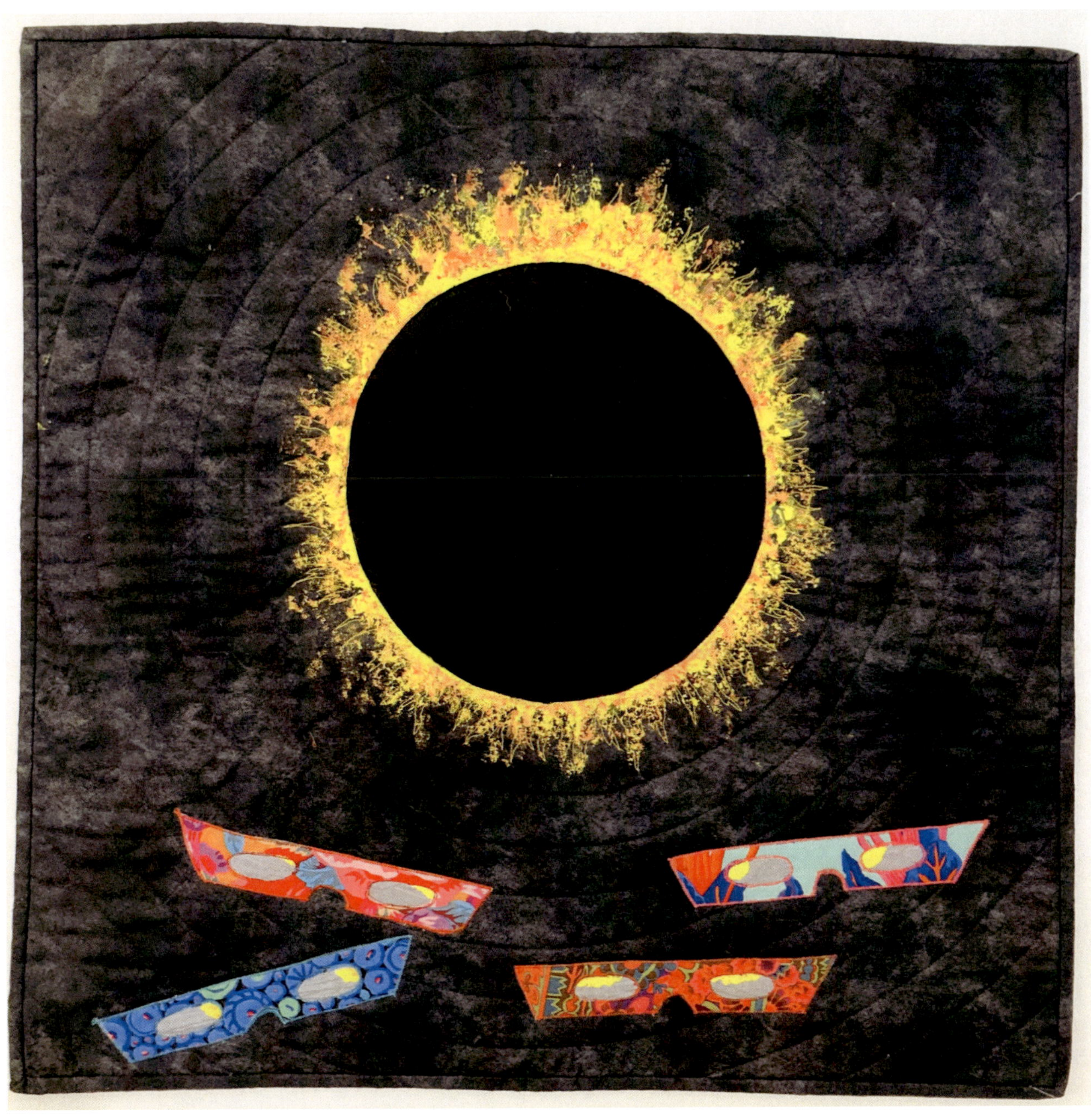

Art Quilt: "I Spy an Eclipse Safely" by Susan Copley Novack

Eclipse Rays by Suntana

Barbara M Linde

Sung to the tune of "Evil Ways" by Carlos Santana

You've got to stop those solar rays, viewer
Before they start hurtin' you.
Protect your eyes, viewer.
So do what NASA says you should do.

You've got to cover and filter with ISO cert.
Don't have a wrinkle, or scratches, or rips that will hurt.
Glasses stay on
'Til eclipse viewing's done.

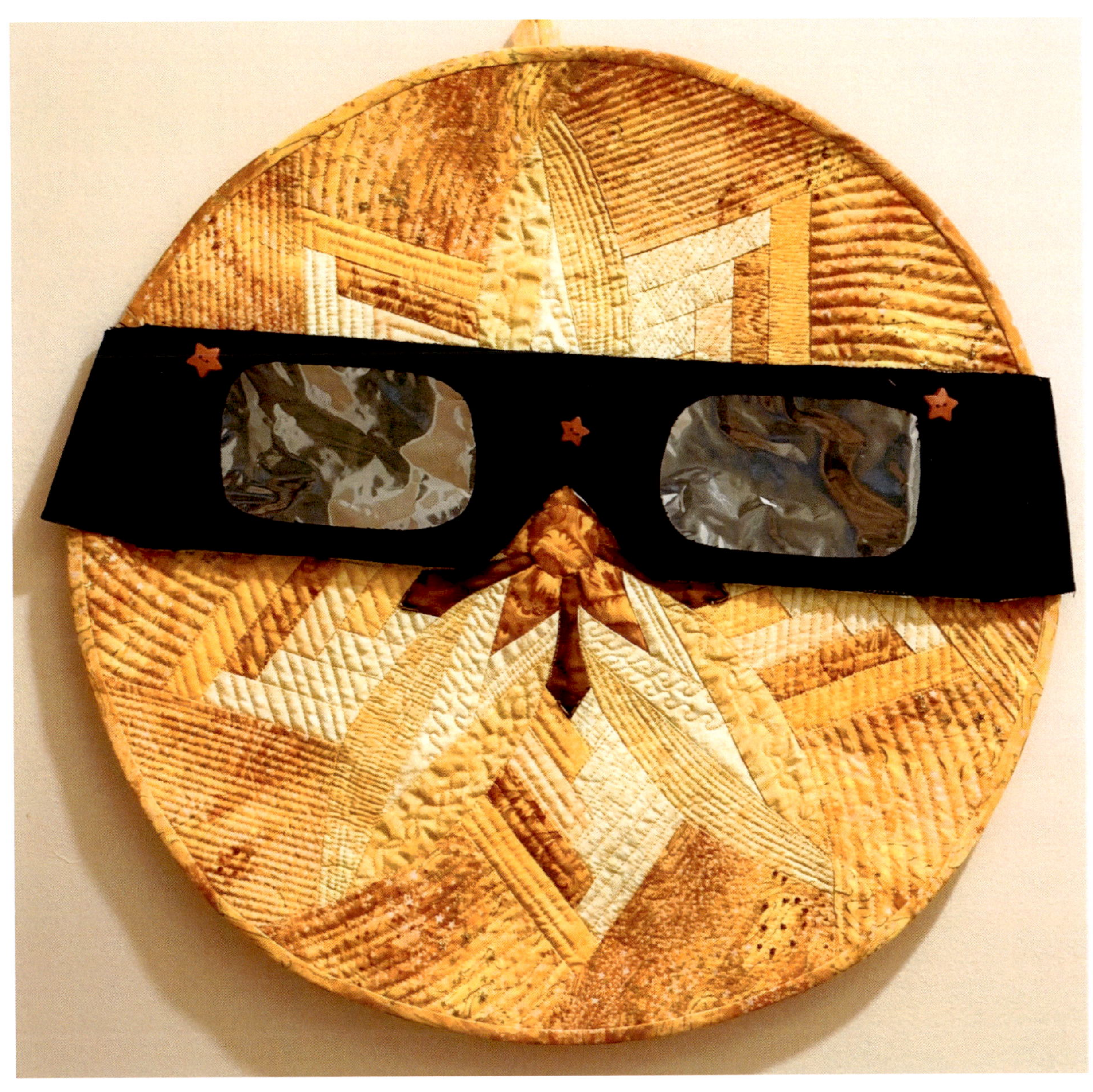

Art Quilt: "Solar Eclipse Glasses" by Barbara M. Linde

SECTION II: GLOBAL EFFECTS

The Colors of Music

Zoey Dudding

I can see it:
the way music dances,
pirouettes,
flaming cardinal notes sashay
via the lop-sided bottoms of their
d & p shaped weights, silently
humming cerulean sentences,
settling
in numbness of their afterglow, inky ebony seeping
through seams of milkwhite lavender, frosted
with chalky, muted silence.
shapeless, formless, more opaque than anything,
beautiful in its brilliance,
nearly choking on the richness of something to soft to taste;
supple, just one spoonful is enough,
music is pliable, malleable,
blush-inducing lushness that sticks in your throat like honey,
syrupy and heavy,
warping sense until all that is left is
the scent of osmanthus.

Ozone Depletion

Holly Panzera

We blamed,

When we started out.

We screamed they had destroyed.

We raised fists in the air,

And our wrists dripped sweat combined with their smog.

Here we are,

Back where we started.

We are colliding with each other

In the vapor and the dark.

No safe haven, no air to breathe, and not knowing

How to work with each other.

A ringlet of sanity creates a slit of sunlight

Through the vapor and darkness.

If we once again believe in science, climbing out to the next planet,

Can the children of our children,

Cleanse the air and breathe

In the morning light?

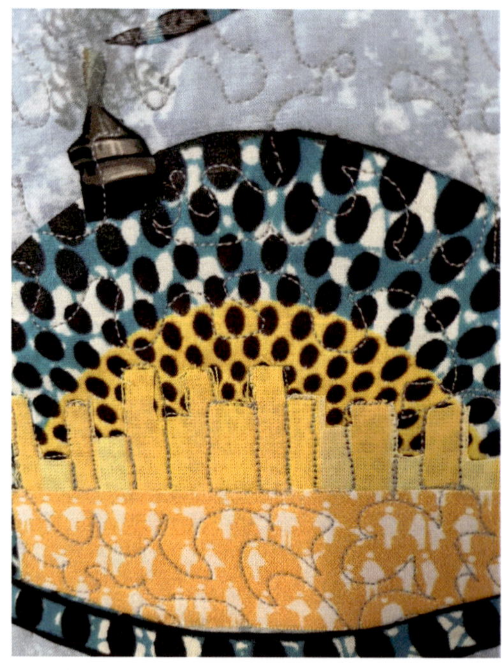

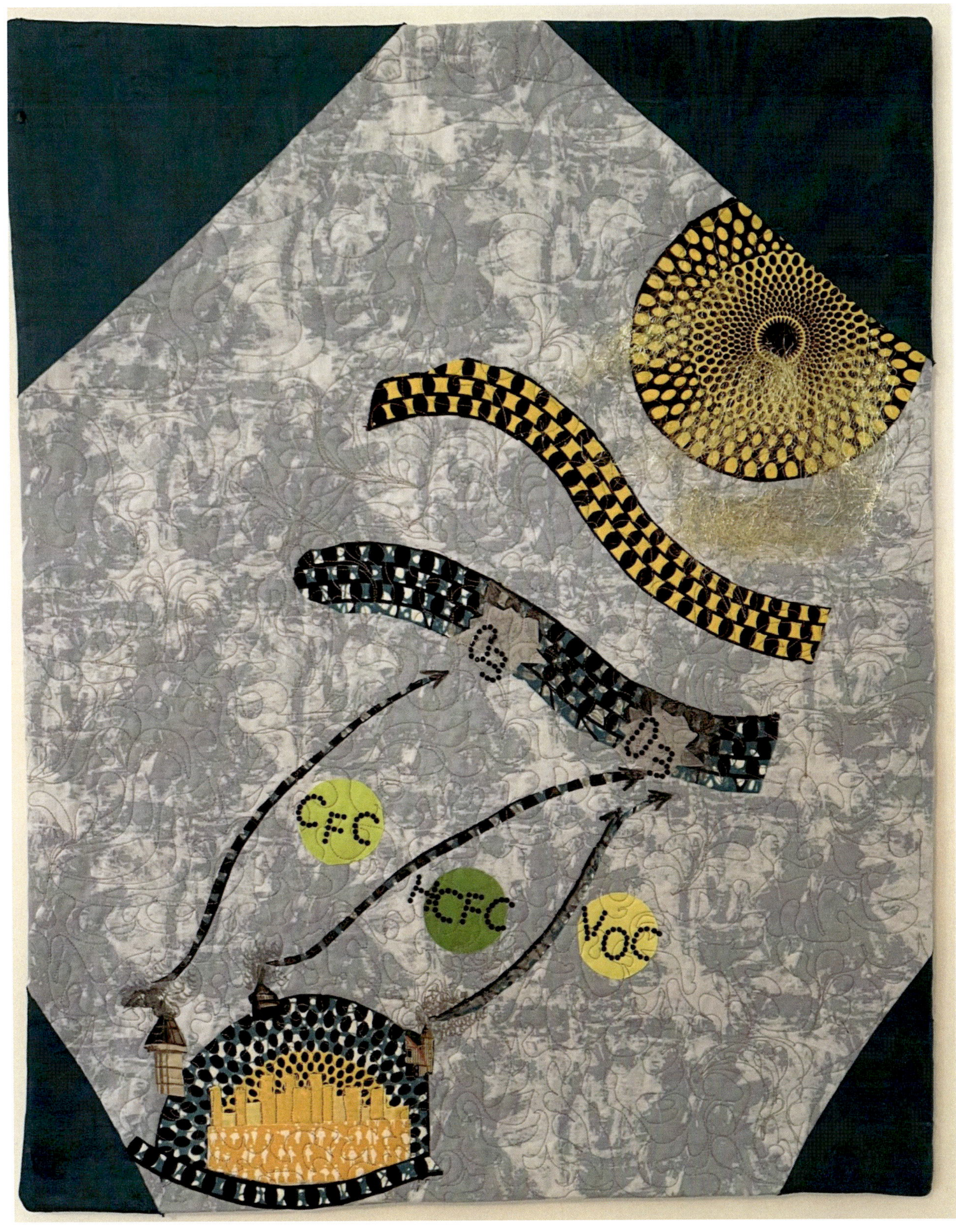

Art Quilt: "Ozone Depletion" by Holly Panzera

A Picture's Testament
Catalina Florina Florescu

This is the polaroid of winter moving
rapidly, forced to admit
...a changing season:
We were here
The earth was holding us tight
...a lovers' embrace
The sky was clear
We were enthralled
We knew of change
...a transformation
We woke up
Thanking
Hoping.
We were here
We existed:
Let the image
Speak
...Frozen in time.

1978 to 1982

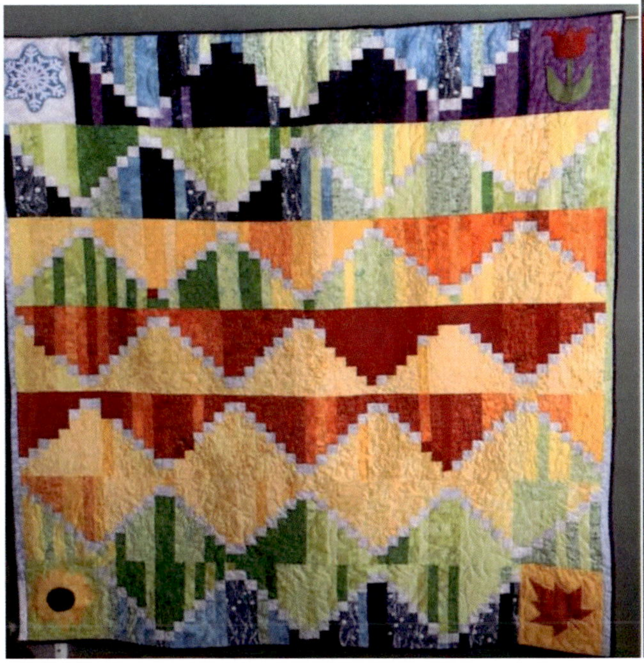

2016 to 2020

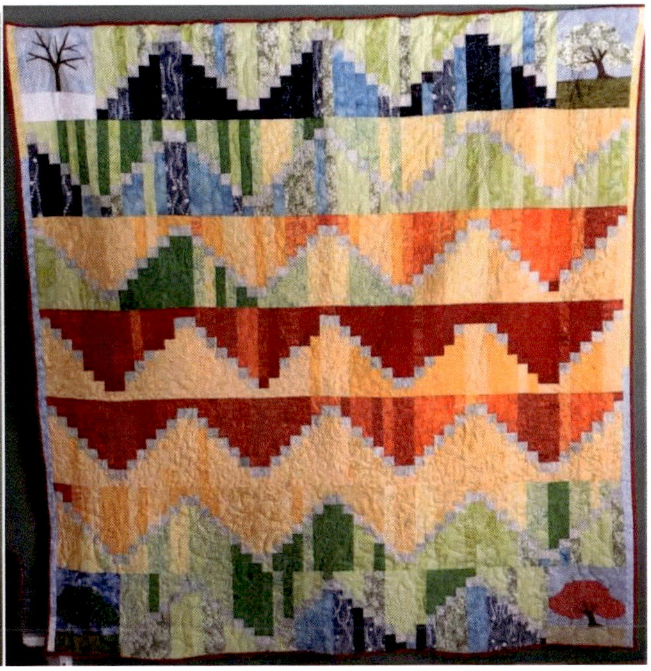

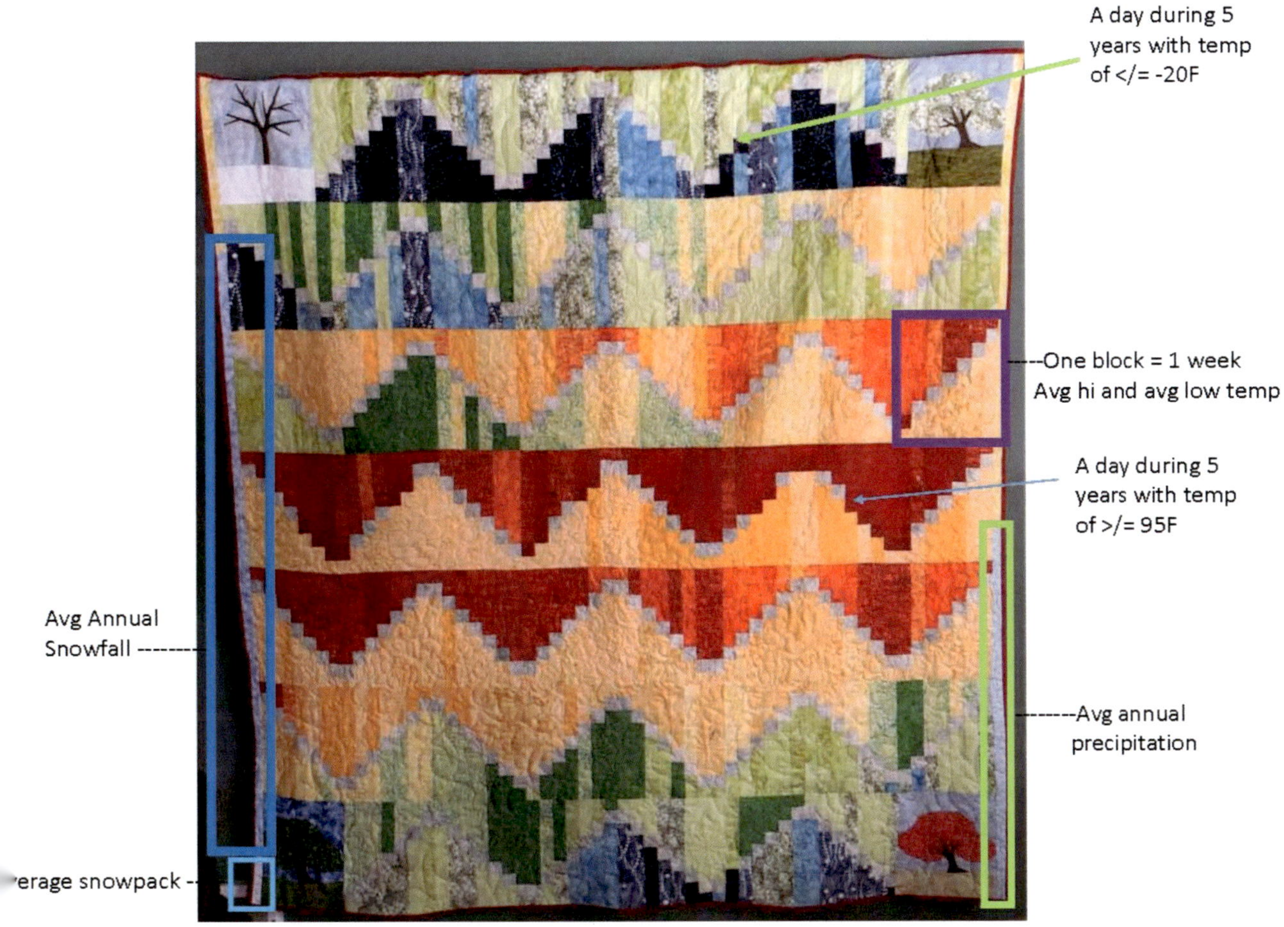

A day during 5 years with temp of </= -20F

One block = 1 week
Avg hi and avg low temp

A day during 5 years with temp of >/= 95F

Avg Annual Snowfall

Avg annual precipitation

erage snowpack

Art Quilt: "Climate Change is Subtle but Fast" by Sarah Parker

Scorch-torn
Megan Brown

The sun splits the sky
like an old wound,
spills fever onto asphalt,
bone, and skin.

A body curls
under a mesquite's thin breath,
tongue thick,
lips cracked open,
scorch-torn and shrieking.

We bottled heat,
let it pool in the throats
of the unhoused
in the hands
of workers bent like dying crops
in the blood
of those chasing escape
into fire.

Time spat us back,
and we redden in its acid,
counting the lost,
names blistered by the sun.

They promise us trees –
ten thousand green beginnings
for those with no place to grow.
Still, the wind carries their dust,
Still, the ground opens its hands.

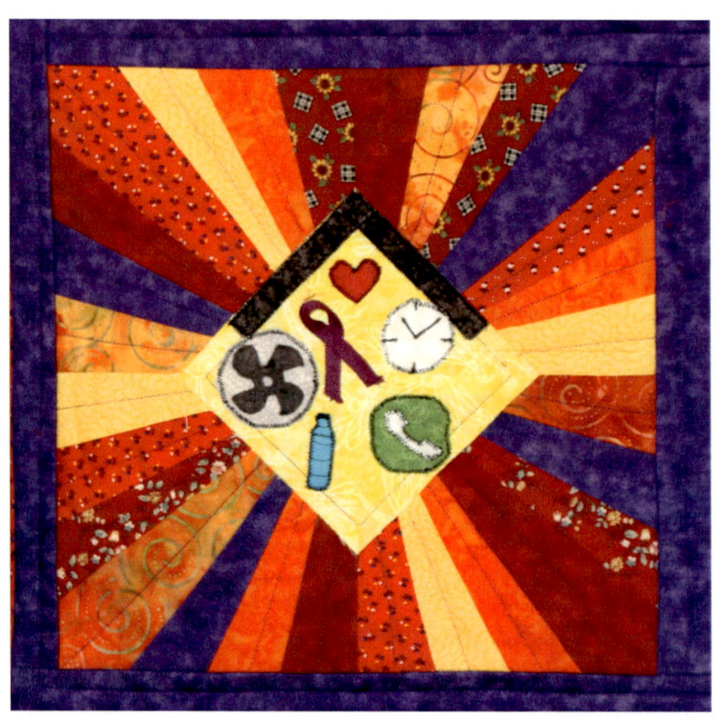

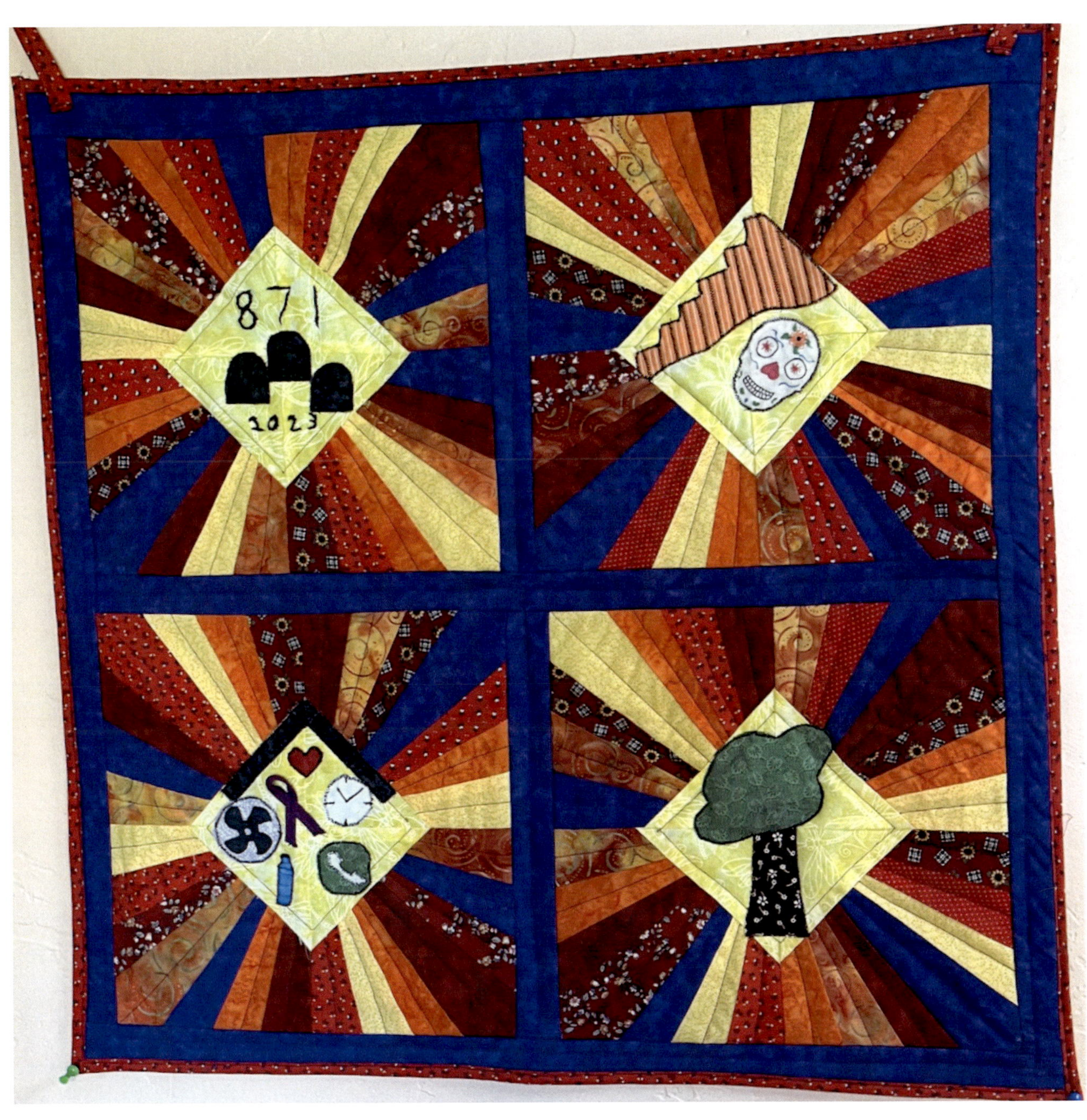

Art Quilt: "Heat Kills" by Betsy Wilkening

Formula on the Floor

Marjorie Gowdy

Newly minted scientist, thrilled as a woman
to interrupt this male paradise of neutrons,
is tasked for the first quarter only with
clean-up after hours.

Hair tied back, she wipes beakers,
polishes glass plates, mops, stands at the
chief's whiteboard and imagines
her very brilliance, unsung.

What's that, under his desk? Her lean arms
reach for a yellowed scrap, her hand wipes
away dust: three symbols in faded pencil.
He discarded this?

She can't use his formula, though tossed.
The abandoned draft, however, recalls a symbol
in scraps of dreams she's stowed silently for years.
Now, onscreen, she designs her own algorithm.

I'll show him in the morning. But instead she
places the crumpled page by his mug with a note: thanks.
She next cleans as required, arranges beakers, dusts, mops,
then grins as the door creaks closed in her fleeing wake.

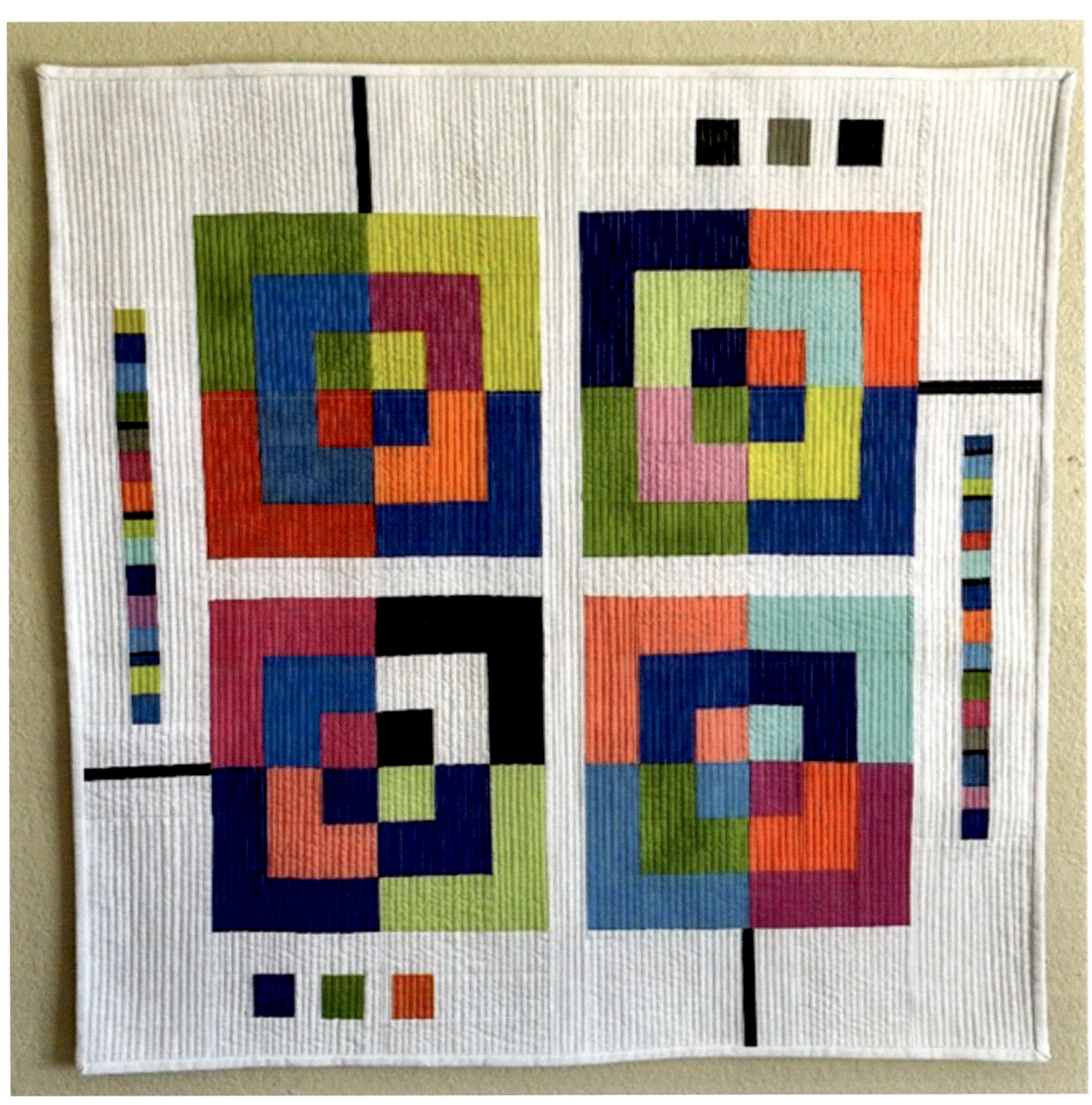

Fiber Art: “Imagining the Unseen” by Lynne Schreiber

SECTION III: CREATURES THAT GO UNSEEN OR UNNOTCIED

Rehoming Bugs

Nicole M. Zwolinski

I watched two women
kill something.

And I am horrified
at my inability to
move.

I sat paralyzed
as they threw
paper towels
over
something
creepy crawly
(I assume.)

And stomp over and over
and over again.

In awe, they were
shocked
that the creature
was still living.

In awe, I was
shocked
that I was still
glued to my bench.

And I hate myself.
for not intervening
and scooping up
the bug and releasing
it outdoors.

Fear, kept me stapled
in place.

I am terrified of
dead things and
the spillage of guts.

And if I didn't see it,
I could pretend it
never happened.

Catawba Mountain

Mattie Quesenberry Smith

Divided and separated, they were the people at the fork Who knew "He-Who-Never-Dies." Did they believe He spoke them out of his sky-mouth onto this deep red clay?

The Catawba people caught fire along His lips and tongue,
And he gave them breath within the cool shadows rising
From the hollows to climb Catawba Mountain. Even today,
We share the same shadows wedged in its clefts. My family
Moved to the foot of Dragon's Tooth Mountain,
Where the road cuts back into Sinking Creek Valley.
They lived off the land on turkeys and deer, squatters
On the edge. Poor, uncivilized Welsh squatters—*the dumbest kind.*

One time I was sitting on Grandma's front porch
On a metal chair, just minding my own business
And watching the kids all running around the yard.
I looked up into the sky, and I entered the mouth of God,
Into a *bona fide* oral cavity. Somehow, I got caught up
In the clouds at sunset. They looked just like God's bright,
Suffering mouth. The clouds rolled together just like
A giant red mouth, complete with both its arches.

Palatine and glossopalatine, I saw the clouds separate as if
They needed to compose His soft and hard palates. I saw
Deep ridges, and it looked a lot like God was suffering or
Yawning in the middle of His closeup conversation or
Vomiting someone out, someone neither hot nor cold.
Is this the same God recognized and transported by
The Catawba people fleeing Canada, "He-Who-Never-Dies?"

None of us will get this story right between the lot of us, but
Filled with blood-red, roiling light, the sky's mouth has been
A cathedral of echoes spelling it out through thunder and light.

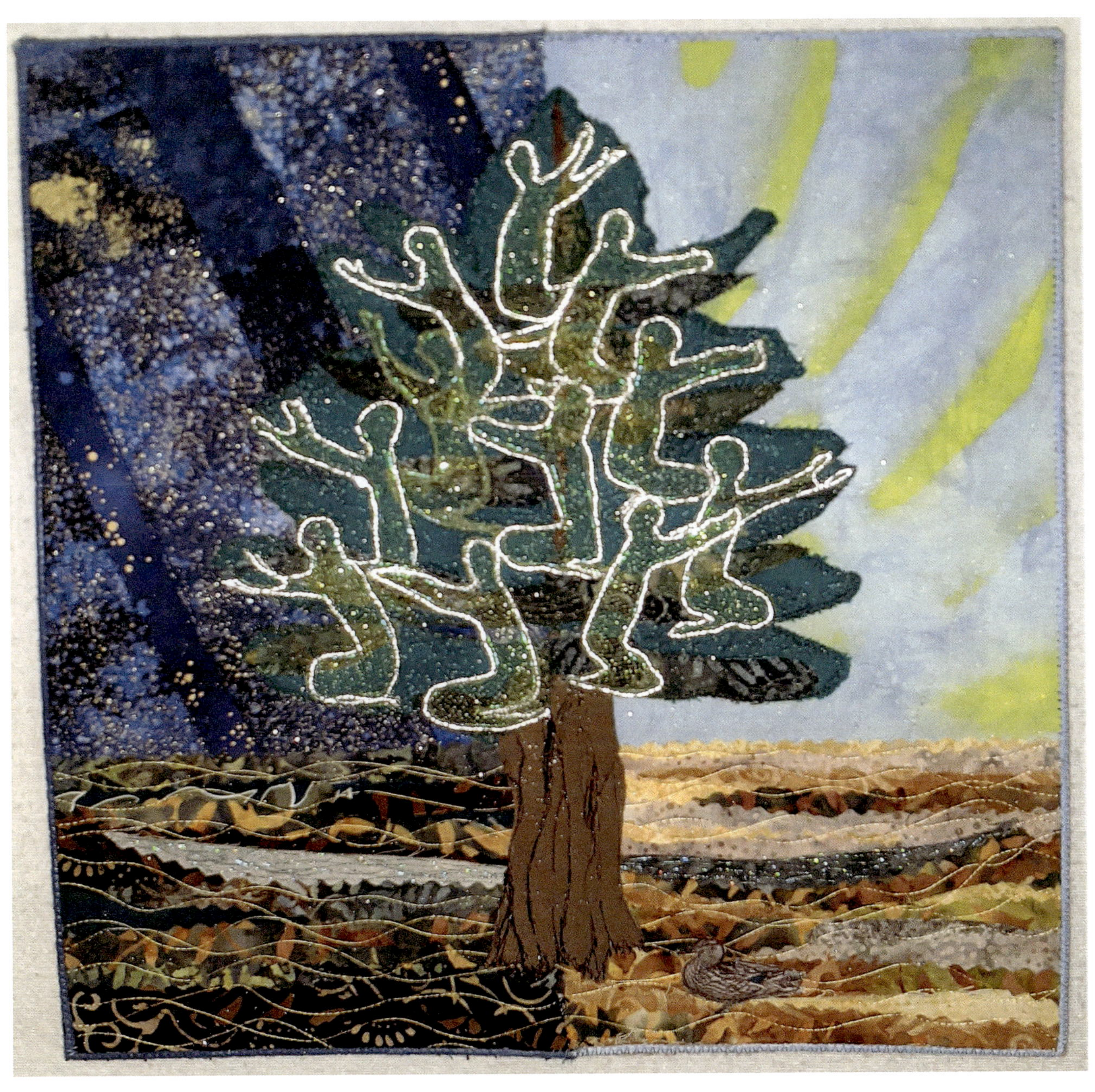

Art Quilt: "Cedar Spirits" by Sally Harcum Maxwell

Vesper Shawl

--a prayer for brown bats

Loralee Clark

A small, furry creature crawled across
the gray, painted floorboards as I bathed;
an errant attic bat, sleep-dazed and wandering.
My grandfather hooked the claw atop her wing
into the tennis racquet string and carried her outside.

May we remember all the soft, tan joys of gradation
their long, thin finger bones knitted into hand-wings.
May we remember all the soft, tan users of
echolocation, bound to its young as we are,
making milk for sustenance.
May we remember all the soft tans wrapping themselves
around our hearts, active in the in-betweens and liminal.

As Venus, the evening star, rises, so do the bats;
glory be for the mosquitos eaten, the countless
itching bites we have been saved from enduring.
Glory be for the dispersing of seeds that replenish
and grow on our lands. For the pollination of flowers,
for regeneration and foods. Glory be
that these chocolate beauties
protect and warm our spirits.

Amen.

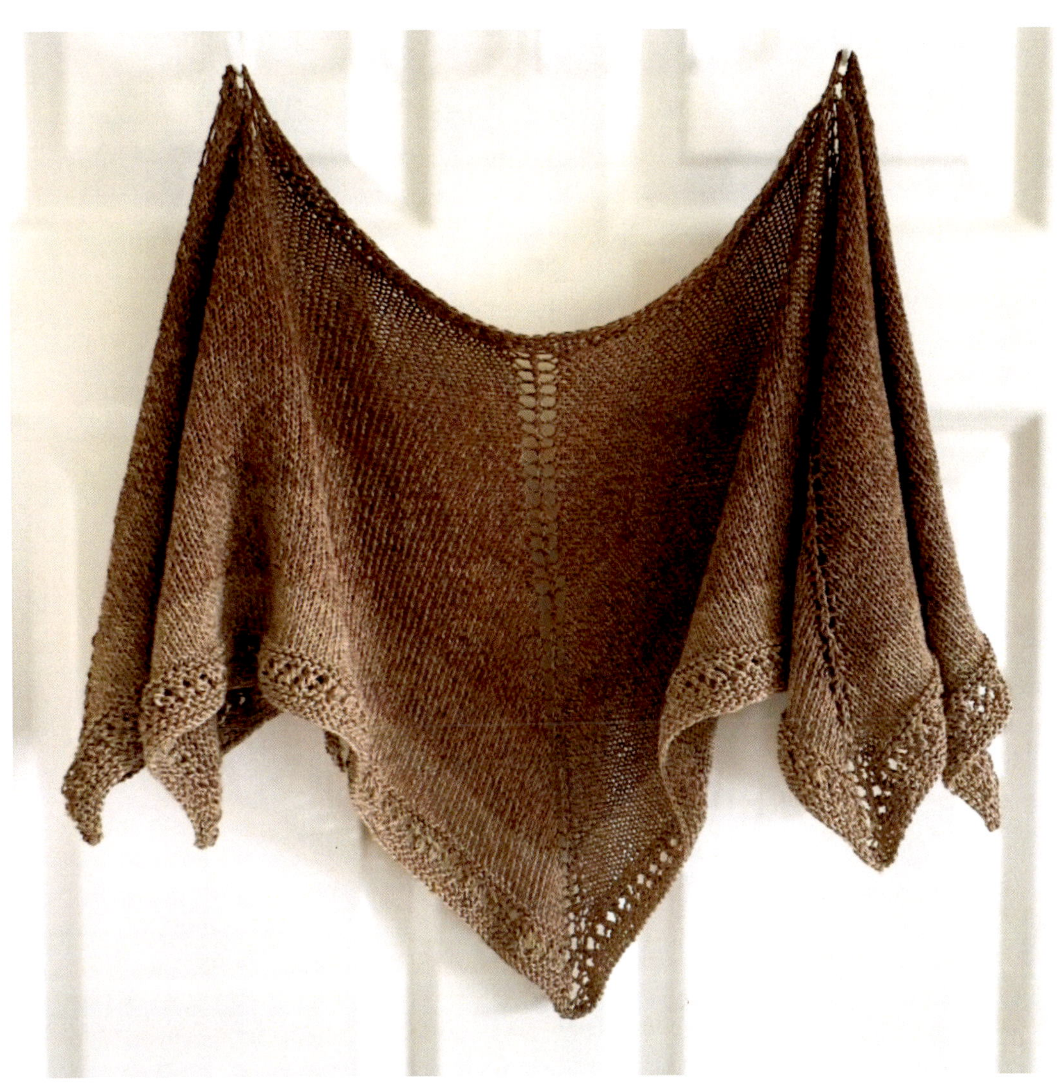

"Vesper Shawl" by Sarah-Beth Bradley

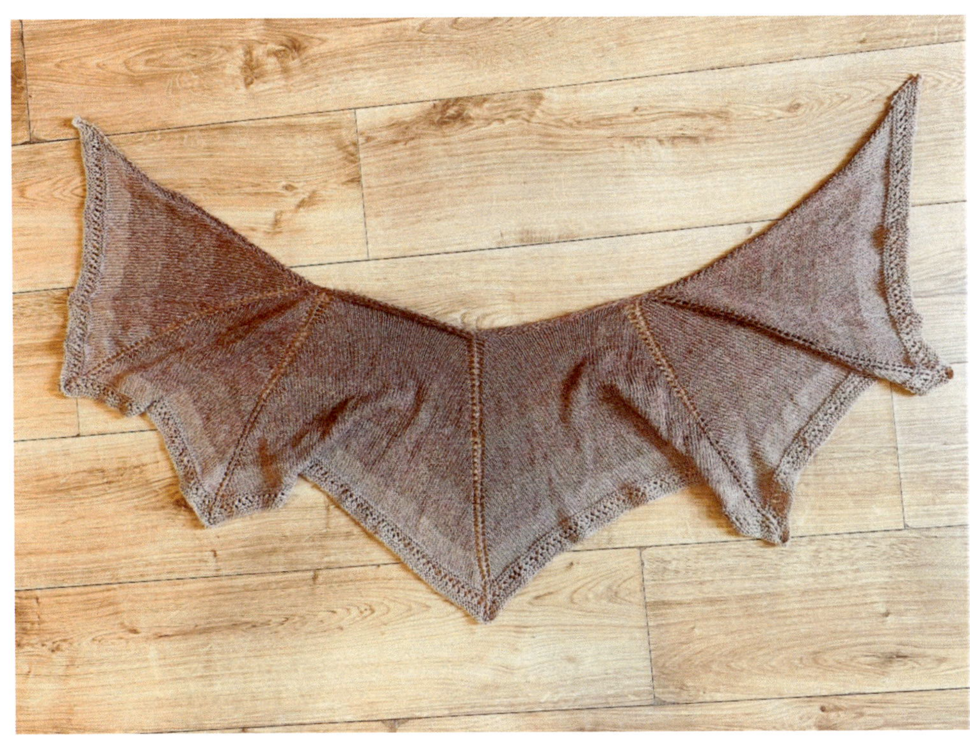

Bellwether for the Wetland Habitats
Carolyn Kreiter-Foronda & *Joyce Brinkman*

Enter the wetlands. Hunt high and low
        for me, a medium-sized butterfly,
tawny-brown with lemony-ringed

black dots on the bottom of my wings.
        Wear boots. In Virginia scour
through mires. Don't let bulrush hinder

your journey. Be like me: determined
        to care about marshy areas
which need help to flourish. Don't let

builders or farmers drain this region.
        My mates sometimes lay eggs
on dead leaves here. Ban herbicides

and pesticides. If toxins spread,
        there's no way we can prosper.
Why capture us? Why kill us in traps?

Why am I important? I'm rare, unique,
        one-of-a-kind. On a trek
through states, you might spot a few

Mitchell's satyr butterflies in southern
        Michigan, Maryland, Alabama,
Mississippi, but in only one county

in Virginia. If you protect my species
        by refusing to destroy wetlands,
you will aid me, as well as other insects,

such as pine tree crickets and red-legged
        spittlebugs. Remember. You, too
can confront challenges by embracing

the divine freedom to flit away from life's
        obstacles. We all have the right
to go on living in safeguarded realms.

Enter wetlands

        on

                your journey.

Ban toxins!

                Why kill

                        one-of-a-kind?

Mitchell's satyr butterflies

        protect,

                confront challenges.

Embracing

        divine freedom

                in safeguarded realms.

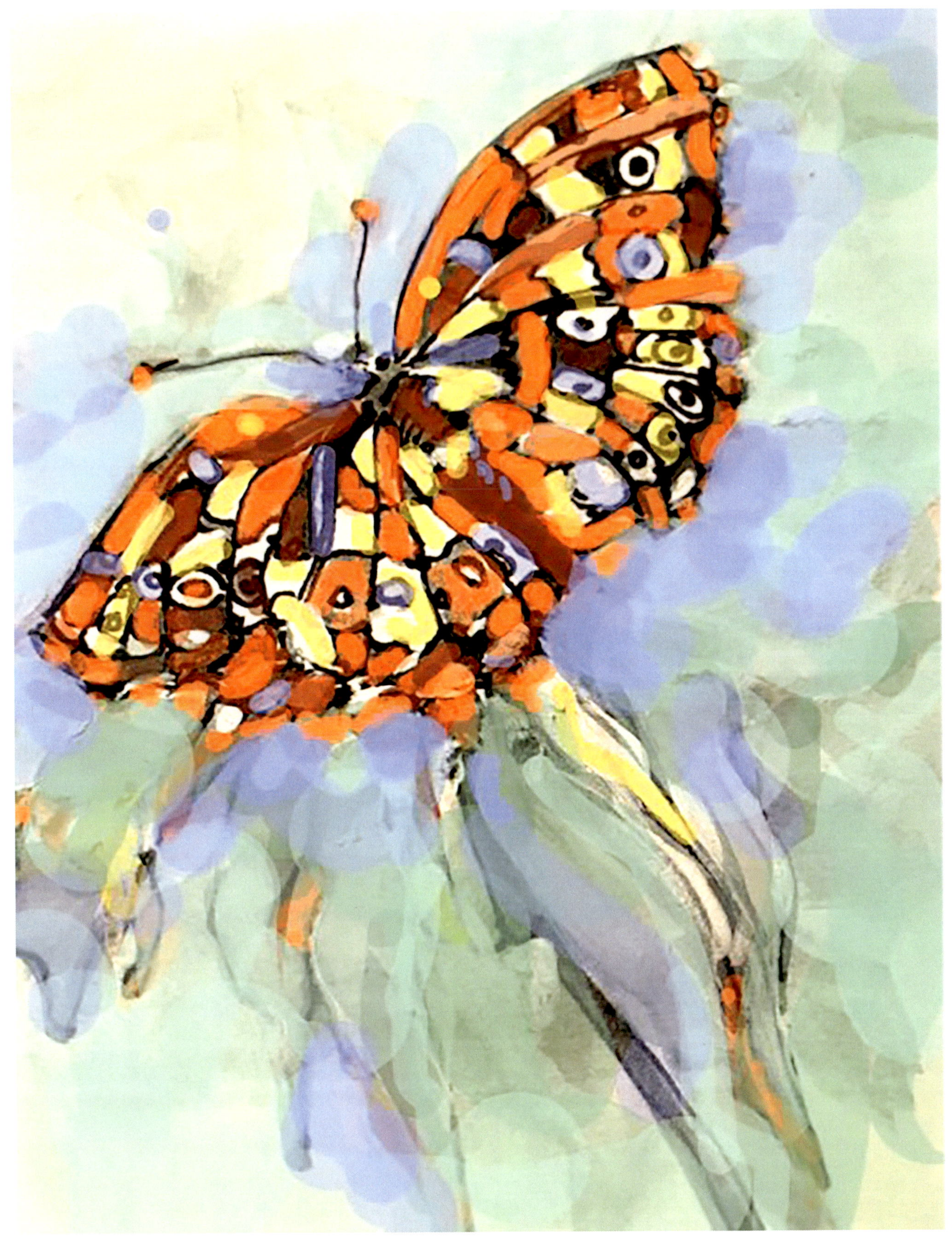

Watercolor: "Fritillary" by Marjorie Gowdy

How Seagulls Are Affected by Sugar Tax

Samantha Carr

With his white weighted feathers
and his sea salted glisten,
the seagull soared above two
legged destiny, wings spanned
on delicate pockets of air.
His food Poseidon's gift,
Nereid laden silver platter -
life was sweet, hovering on
thermals, snoozing on sharp cliff.

Poseidon's gifts were salty,
like his temper and our
yellow footed friend sought
sanctuary on land. Stolen
scraps from sandy shores,
he became an ice cream cone
connoisseur, adopted a sweet
centred palate and oh,
how he dreamt of chips.

His gull call hasn't sung
sea tales, no sailors walking planks,
drunken shipwreck rocks,
things lost to the brine of time
at the bottom of a rocky alcove.
Our white feathered friend
hasn't flown for a while, as carb
cravings occupy his watchful
side eye gaze.

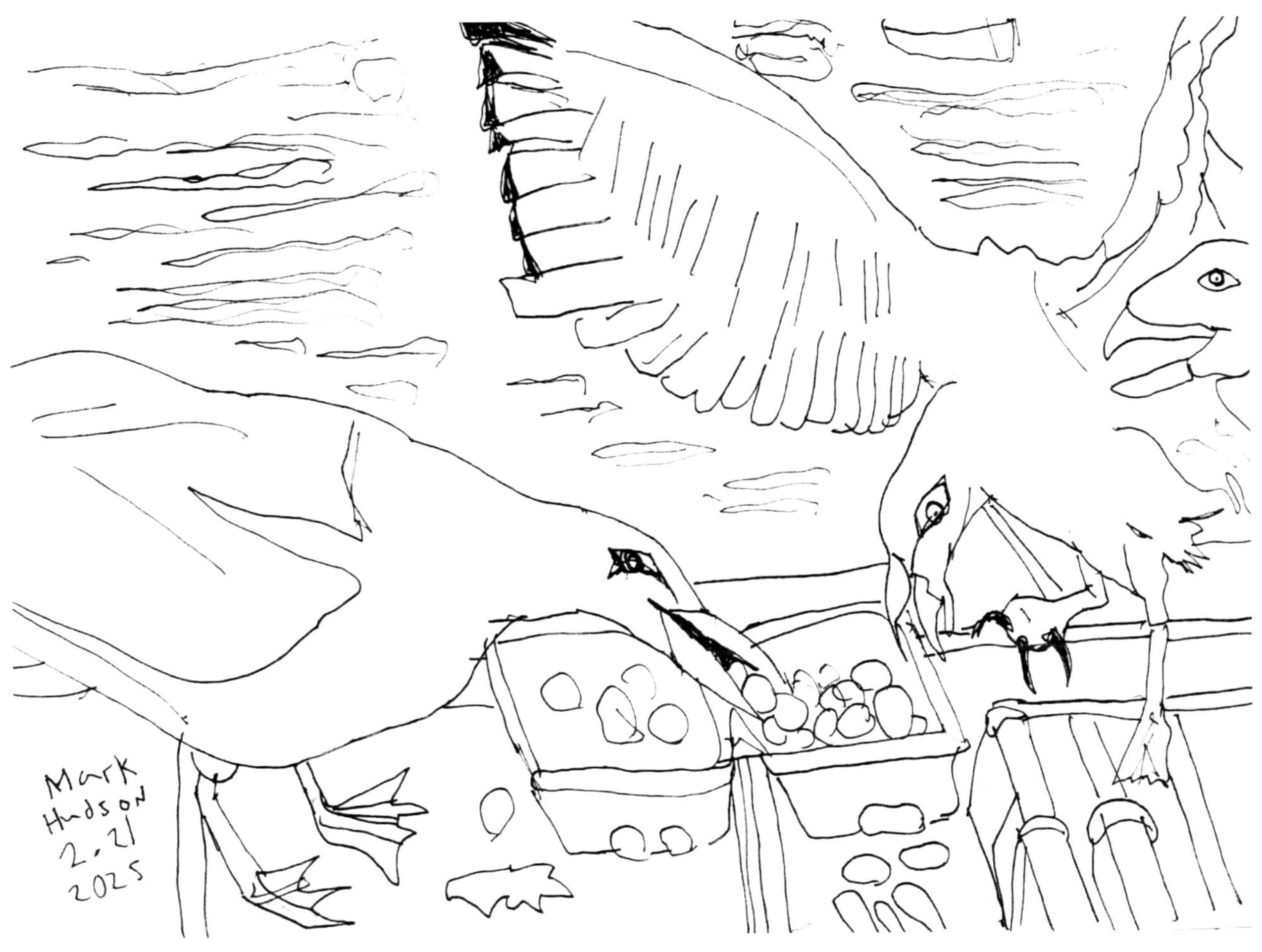

Drawing: "Seagulls Dumpster Diving" by Mark Hudson

The Pied Piper's Song

Samantha Carr

He banished the mice to the river,
playing pop songs on repeat
until their tiny ears and tiny tails
could bear it no more.

The river's wet, winding
secrets embraced the little
critters. They made their lives
in discarded shopping trolleys.

They tormented the fish,
with their cruel jokes about
gills, and scales as though wet
fur coats were any better.

We thought they'd fight back –
the proud trout at least, but
they never did. Sleepy with
sewage spill pill residues.

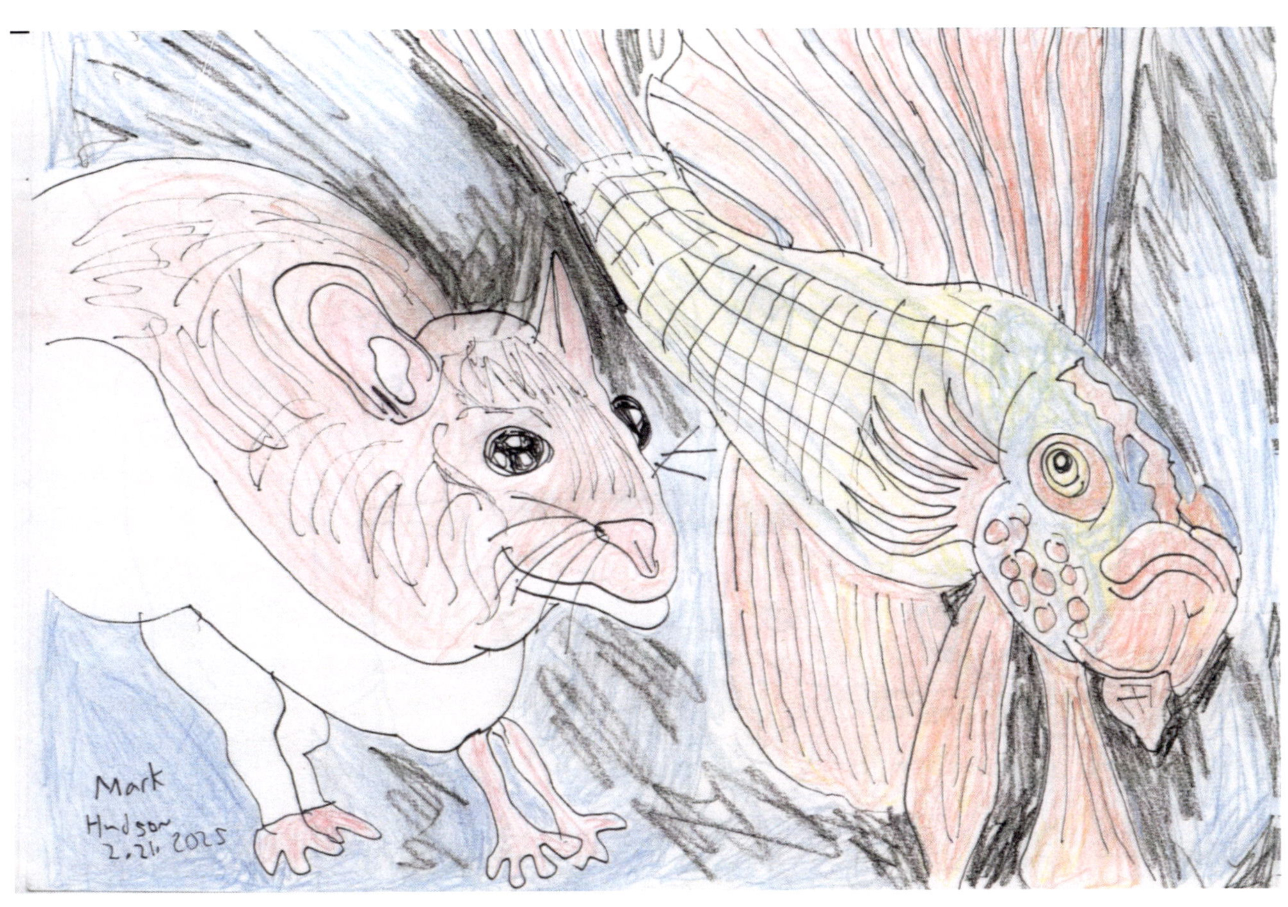

Drawing "Toxic River Denizens" by Mark Hudson

In Defense of the Possum
Marjorie Gowdy

At differing latitudes, across a continent,
the agony of the snow-less collapses
in the same keening of animals now sleepless
clawing out of muddy dens once pristine
into a landscape changed by the greediness
of men.

Hail to the moose and great gray owl and snowshoe hare
as to their cousins here the black bear, screech owl, and red-winged hawk.
Fortitude sought for the majestic firs along once-frozen
northern lakes and to Virginia pines snapped
in adolescence by unfettered ice
breaking willfully.

The opossum here, the opossum there
so misunderstood before and after the climate's change,
simply seeking insects we loathe and
seeds we discard as the best of meals
for a humble featureless creature
lacking a friend.

I'd save them all – I'm old and save spiders now,
if I could and if we all would but humans on
screens big and small grow careless
among the deep woods of green dollars.
The radical in me lashes out at these selfish men,
but the possum in me hoards my own circle of seed.

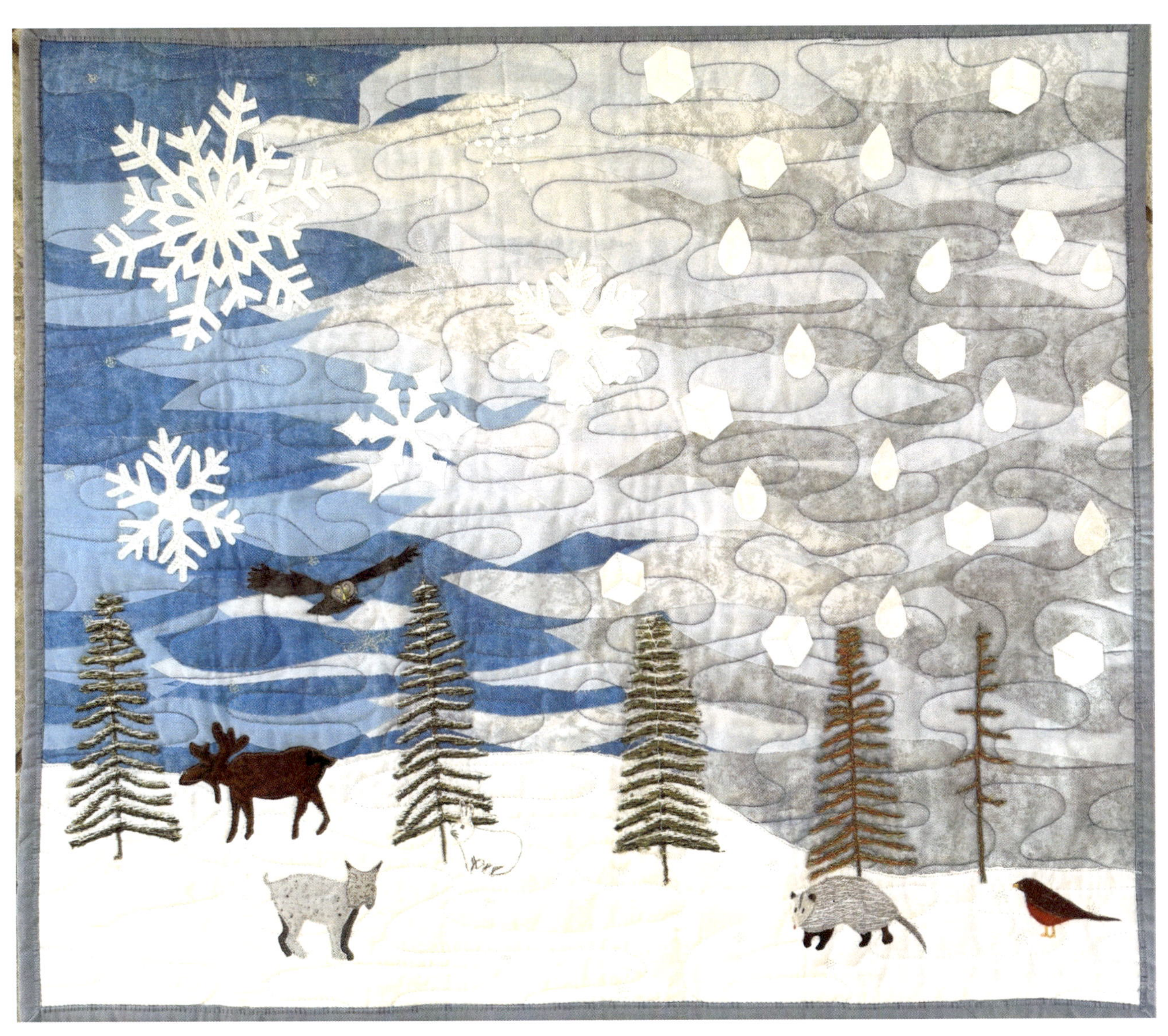

Art Quilt: "A Changing Season: by Sarah Parker

The Sumatran Tiger Sounds Off
Carolyn Kreiter-Foronda & *Joyce Brinkman*

Stop invading my territory.
        Are you trying to capture me?
What happened to my forest?

Without the protection of trees
        it's difficult for my breed
to have babies and survive.

You poacher. You're stalking
        me for my sharp teeth,
claws, skin, bones, and fur

so you can make overcoats,
        rugs, ornamental jewelry
to sell on the black market.

Don't you dare go hunting
        again on land
that's not yours. I'm vulnerable

here on the Island of Sumatra
        because of trespassers
like you. Don't steal my food.

Leave wild pigs, deer, baby
        elephants, and cattle
alone so I can stay healthy.

If you come closer, I'll snarl,
        hiss, and roar
until you can no longer hear.

I'm a solitary animal. I want
        to be alone. If you
engage in illegal logging,

if you destroy my protected
        area and my food supply,
I will vanish into thin air.

Stop invading

        my forest.

                Without trees

it's difficult.

        You poacher,

                black market hunting!

On Sumatra

        leave pigs, deer

                alone.

I'll snarl,

        hiss,

                roar.

A solitary animal

        I want to be

                alone.

You destroy.

        I will vanish

                into thin air.

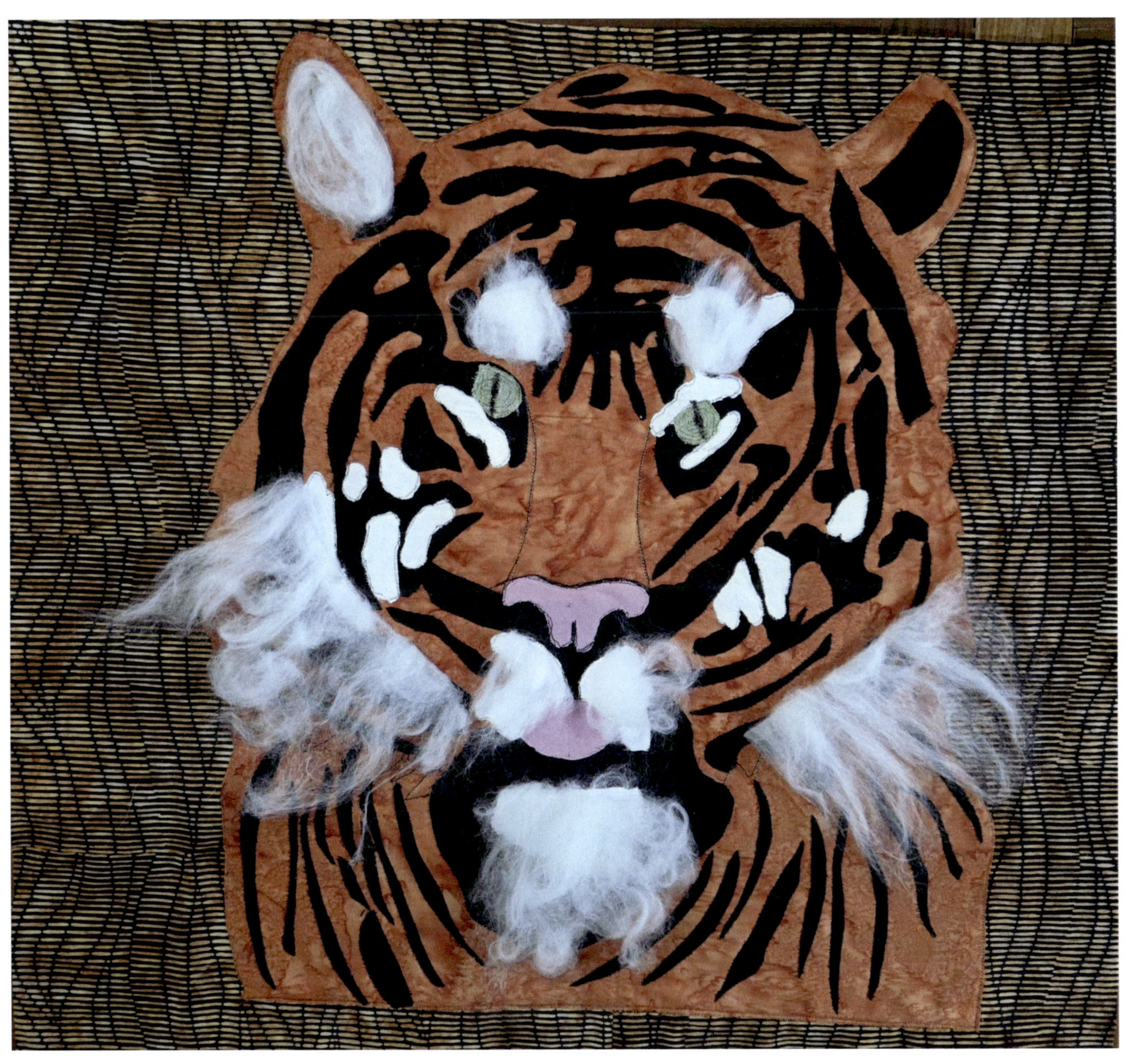

Art Quilt: "Sumatran Tiger" by Kerry Faraone

How Doth the Toxic Crocodile

Samantha Carr

Here we see the toxic crocodile swimming through the tyre-ridden river where nothing is supposed to thrive. His ancient eyes mock scientists as they collect samples with their latex covered hands. His soft underbelly resting in cool mud as the sun's rays filter through exposed skies. Legs splayed – he looks relaxed, ready for a nap maybe. But did you know this side-to-side sweep can reach eleven miles per hour? How fast the river fills with bacteria spills we can never outrun. Halitosis greets us as we pootle on past in our tourist boat. The stale stench of a rotten keep of foraged food doesn't bother him. *How cheerfully he seems to grin* as we glide by – he doesn't mind lying in wait in our human waste if we drop in sometimes.

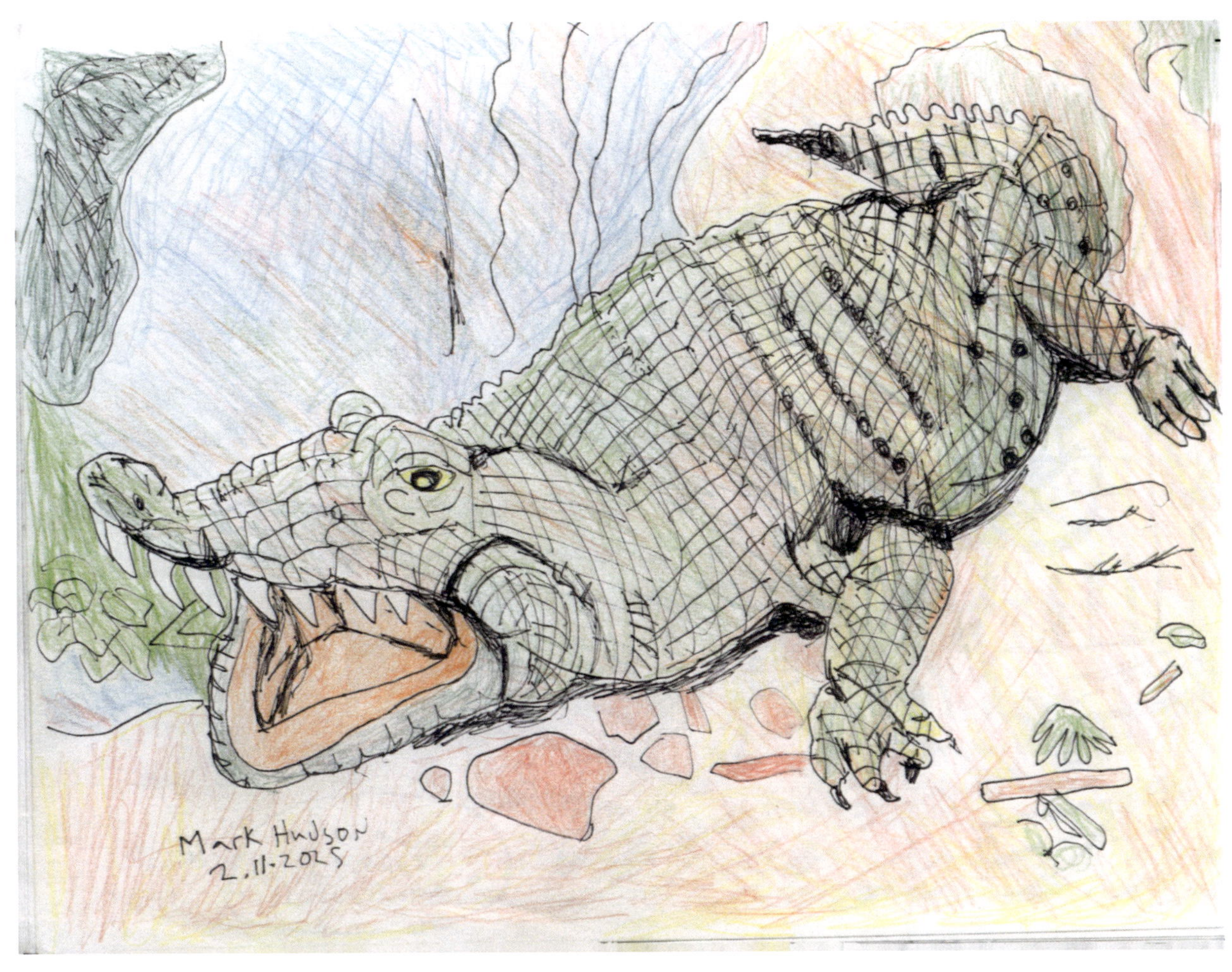

Drawing: "Crocodile" by Mark Hudson

Mud Dauber Wasp Nest
R. J. Keeler

That little yellow dauber wasp
worked and flew until it dropped.
Until the end of every blessed day
it flew straight, never lost its way.
Found the dirt, mixed the water,
hefted tiny gobs, daubed the mortar.
Never wondered if this mixture
might represent some wider picture—
some perfect mix of *form* and *function*.

Function—raise a progeny within asylum.
Form—daub a ball, a safer nest, a quiver.
Is this a bumbling wasp's ancient elixir,
or ordained by phylum's older nature?
Some Yung Dynasty's expert woodcarver
captured that monk's hot blaze of mystery.

But dauber wasps are *born* consistent—
born enlightened—carry water carry mud;
no need to prize a finger off far-off moons.
It knew well its place in time and space;
no need to plan on how to find a grace.

But then it found a perfect final resting bed—
a nest inside a monk's empty wooden head.
A leavened monk stares off beyond rare air;
but essences of tiny wasp beat him there.

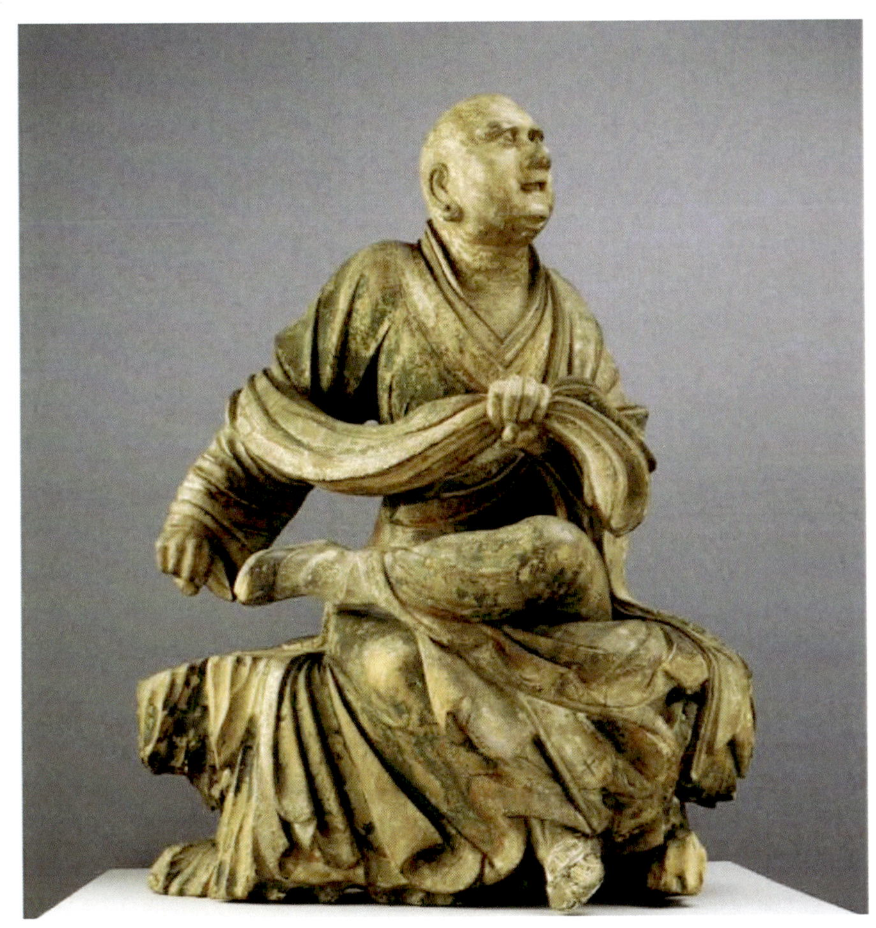

Monk at the Moment of Enlightenment
Wood carving, Seattle Asian Art Museum

A Young Flemish Scientist in Early Contemplation of Gravity and Light*

R. J. Keeler

...I saw it yesterday again—again.
Aloft, mending a transept split by winter ice,
the steeplejack's felt hood blew clean away.
I counted and paced; two, then three, next four.
On five, it skimmed a puddle of melt.
My count and pace were five; the same, exact
same, count of five a shattered brick felled
to earth, to God; the pastor's cow last May
when sun unglued that frozen eastern cornice.
What drew my heeding, my father's inward gulp

...five then; five now. So, were I to fling
this pitcher down, would cream and brass—how odd—
alight at once? My maid could count. No, better I....
My father, bless him, disagrees. Says we counted faster;
nay, counted wrong. But did my heart not beat
to keep that pace? Small matter!

...ah, precious, this chiseled window's beveled edge,
admitting red and blue and royal purple tints.
Just an instant's touch, a breath, amends this patent fan.
But whence? The sun's but yellow. The sky, but blue.
My headdress, white. The table's rug, red. That steady fire,
our sun, so piques my curiousness. A furled anagram?

...well, this Spring, our windowmaker's back.
I'll ask, delicately, would he craft for me
a private bar of clearest glass and sharpest bevel?
For a few guilders? Father, perhaps ...?

...again, that shattered brick. Again, I see its arc
from cornice down to cow. I chart its flight.
Ah, that tinted fan of light—Lord, those selfsame arcs...."

*This poem was first published in *Orbis International Journal* in 2019 .

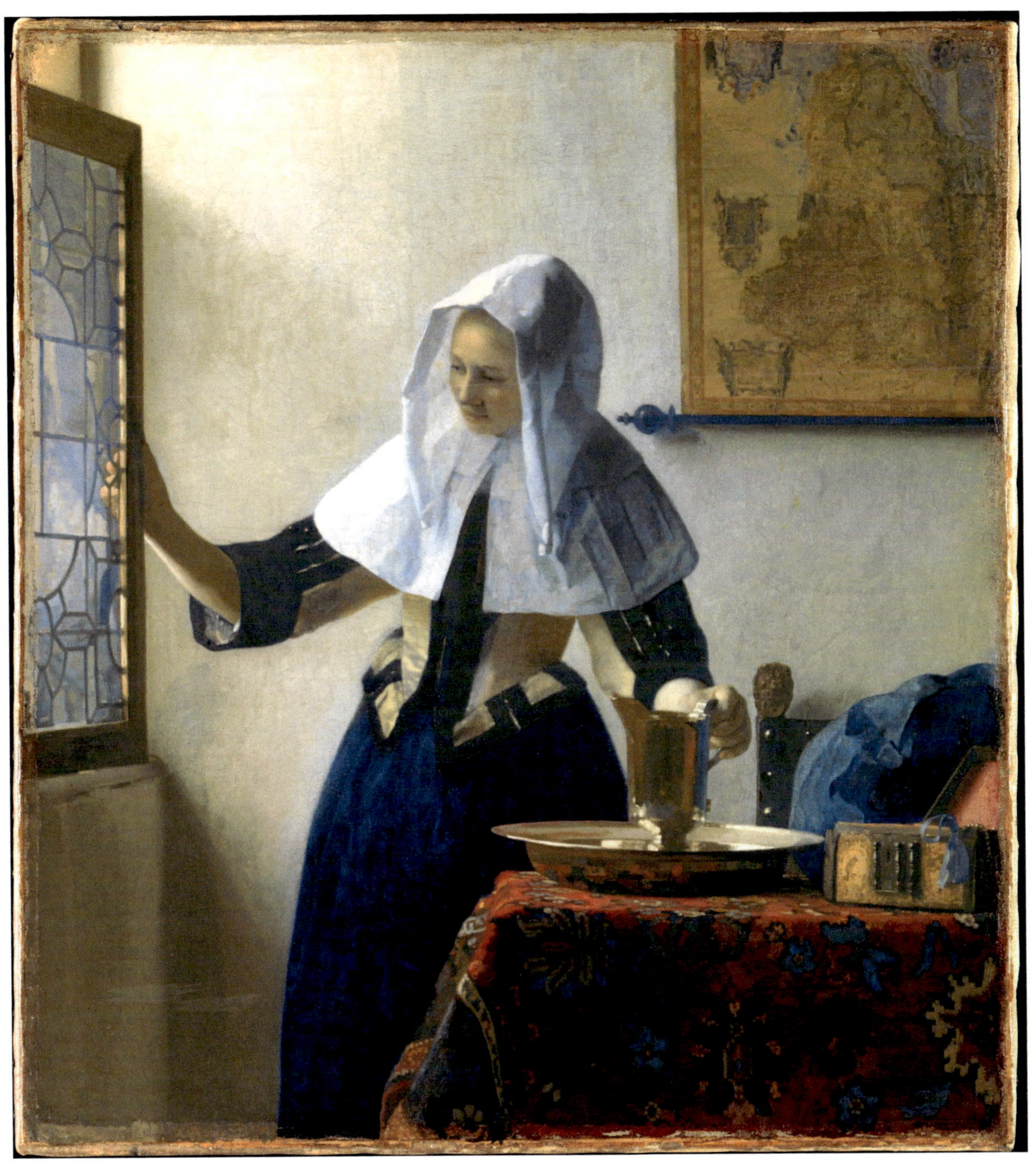

"Young Woman with a Water Pitcher" by Johannes Vermeer

Snow Begins at the End of the World

Ron Smith

At first I wasn't sure—
pale flicks sometimes rising,
white floaters cavorting
where my secret black ones
should be, these frolicking pinprick whiteouts
devising pure space, that living unseen
I forget to account for.
Volume made visible.
Then, the frank delight of fat flakes,
parachuting into a murder of backyard crows
on the disappearing healthy green
of the exorbitant grass
I have not yet killed.

I open windows to make the crows rise
like the slo-mo nightmare of a street blast,
dropping insults as they weave away
into the quiet neighborhood.
I close the windows on the cold.
And now the sprayed burst of a
cardinal's shriek, tapering squall of a red shouldered hawk.
Good to be a writer, close to the coffee,
able to fling off the snarling complexity
of an obstreperous novel
and spend an hour luring the snow
into my tiny notebook.
On the kitchen tiles, yesterday's Times screams
crimes over and over on its front page,
smothering still in clear plastic, vile deeds
typeset just before deadline
and superseded before they can blacken my hands.

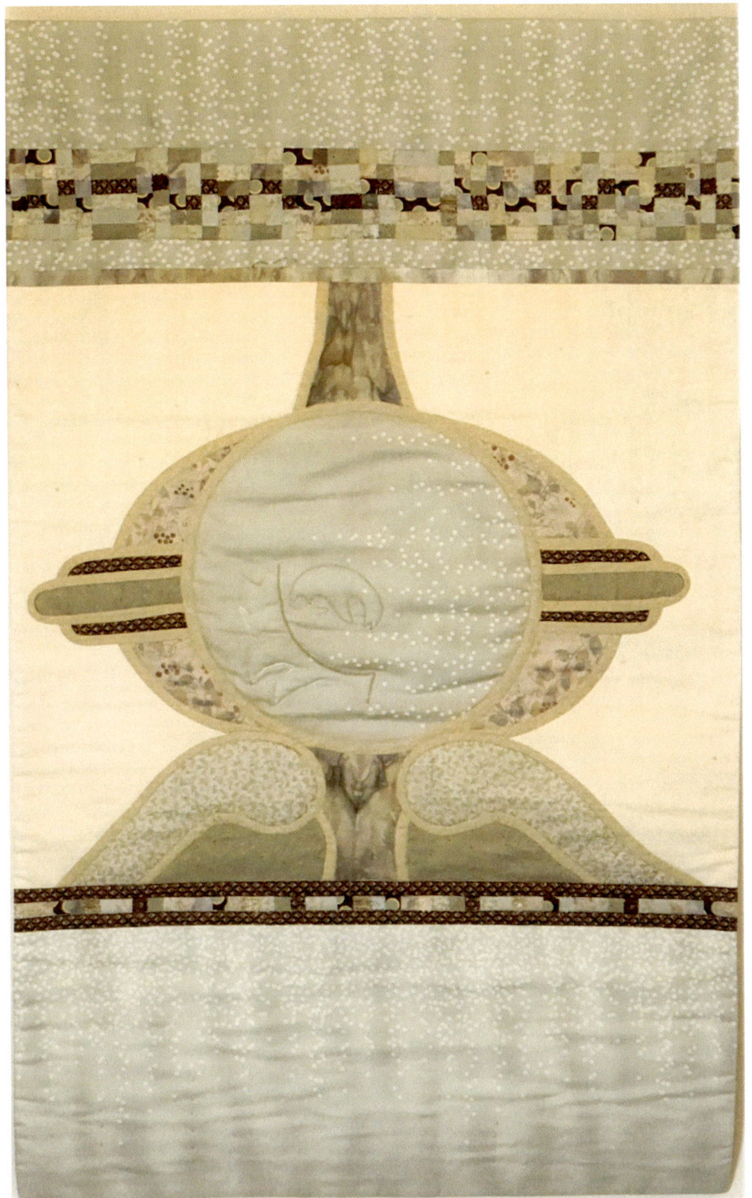

Art Quilt: "Frosty Snowfall" "by Jody Gruendel

And still the snow comes down,
spectral snow that thickens the sight,
emptiness somehow every color of the rainbow.
Nothingness is always something.
They said a storm was on its way,
that we could all lose power.
Beyond the mailbox, the asphalt street
has grown as white as my head. *

*This poem was first published in *Plume*.

Ground's Breaking

Mattie Quesenberry Smith

If wildflowers grew here,
The slate could not slice sunlight
And frustrate our soil breaking.

We could take the time to skip
Along the ground and dig with hoes
Instead of sharp-tipped picks.

Instead, we hopscotch from slate slabs
To stone. Our fire-burned feet slap
Where the trapped sun fails.

Yes, breaking this field will be hard,
But afterwards, we will harvest
Hand-tilled foods from this place.

We will recover a vegetative retreat
Brimming with soft soil and bordered
By a stone wall, full of fresh flowers.

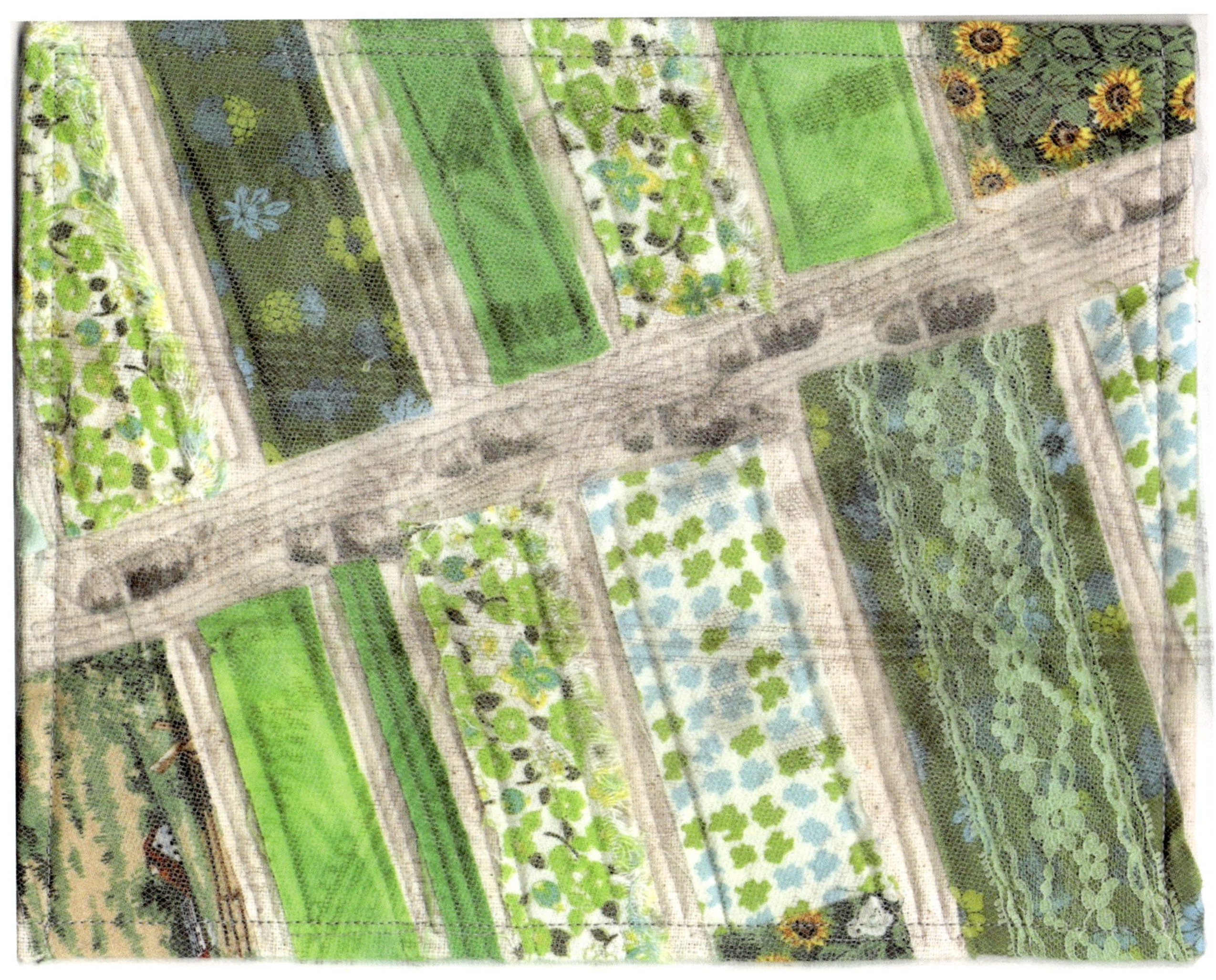

Art Quilt: "Family Farm" by Sally Harcum Maxwell

Carbon Footprints

Anna Isabella Fratarcangelo

We can't see our own organs,
our hearts beating against our ribcages,
our lungs breathing like treetops in wind.
We will never know if our hearts are
perfect fists or our lungs the texture of sponge.
If we did, we would be dying.

The colonists wrote that the rivers in America
ran liquid crystal, that you could see through
the schools of chum to the dusty white floors.
The air, they said, was crisper than Britain's,
untainted by man and his machinations, clean.
Now, I, an American, barrel down the highway daily,
ticking up to my quota as another ton of
greenhouse gasses pours from my car's exhaust.

In India, schoolchildren shield themselves with
handkerchiefs draped across their palms,
squished to their noses. Synthetic fog
looms around them, collecting in the
pores of the pavement beneath their feet.
The grey catches in their hair gel,
the black fabric of their uniforms.
They can see what they breathe,
what hazes anything in front, and what
their loafers press into the path they pass.

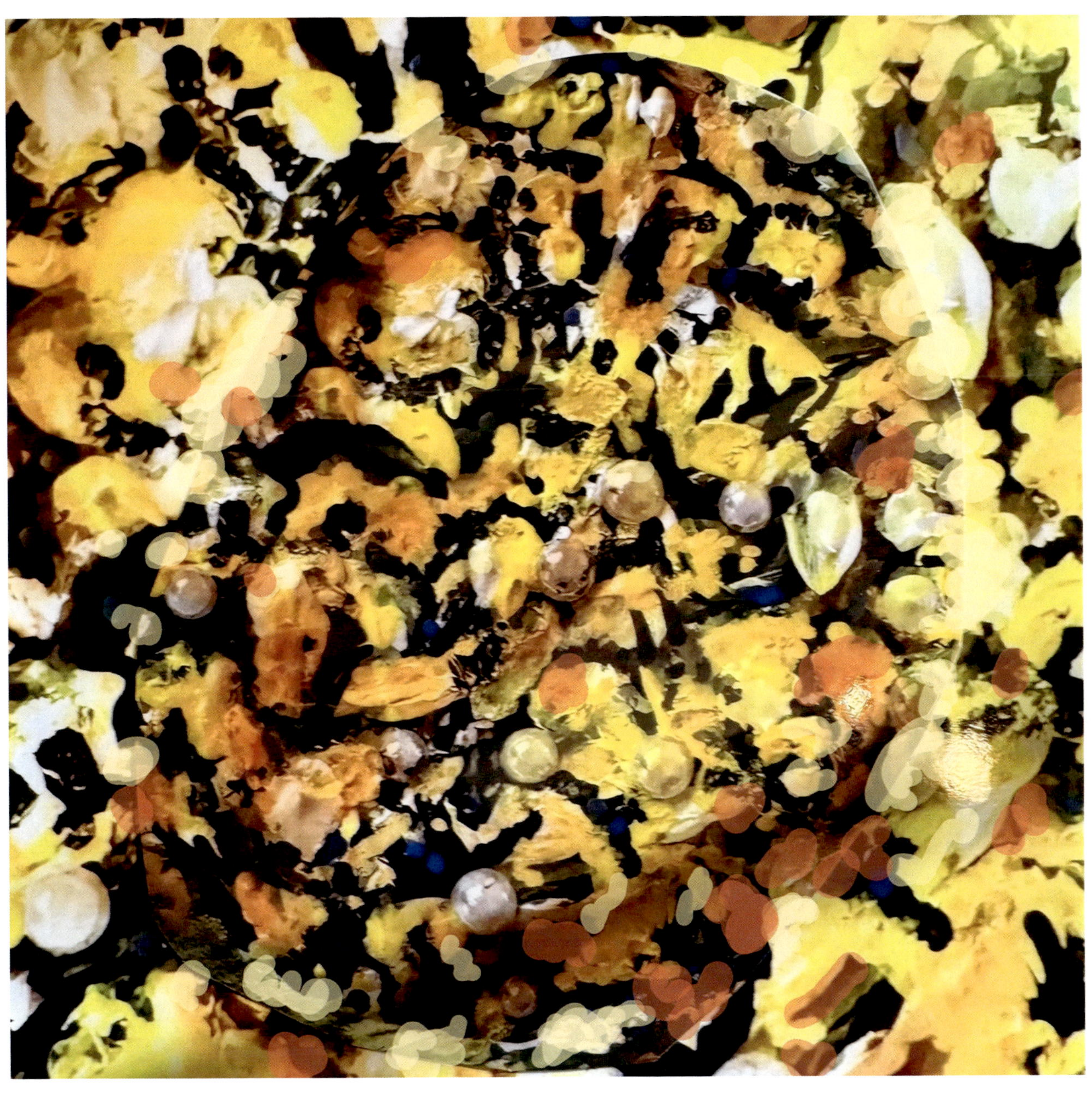

Mixed Media: "The Tortoise is Here" by Marjorie Gowdy

Splay Tree

Mattie Quesenberry Smith

Splayed, listen, here it is: Birth. Stay away from death.
No matter how splayed you are, keep cutting back
To the root. That's what I'm hoping happens
Each time I look for you.
In my dream, I am climbing the tree, Deciduous, coniferous, what does it matter?
I am climbing the tree, in iterations of ascent,
But the tree, it rotates limb from limb,
And each time I grab a branch, I am limb for limb,
A left child and a right child, sinister, then good;
I am the left child of a right child, right child of a left
Child, blind to sinister. I am the left child of a left child,
Twice sinister, and I am the right child of a right child,
Getting back to the root. To get back to the root,
I have to climb the tree. Call it balance. Call it
Recalling the beginning node. Call it searching for you, Father.
Call it coming home to claim my birthright before I am born.
When I was born, I was falling, flailing,
Splayed, fingers from palm, arms from belly,
Legs from groin, toes from sole, grabbing for a limb,
Waiting for a name, hoping for amortization.

This poem was first published in *Phi Kappa Phi Forum, vol. 99, no. 4, pp. 29-30. Honor Society of Phi Kappa Phi, 2019.*

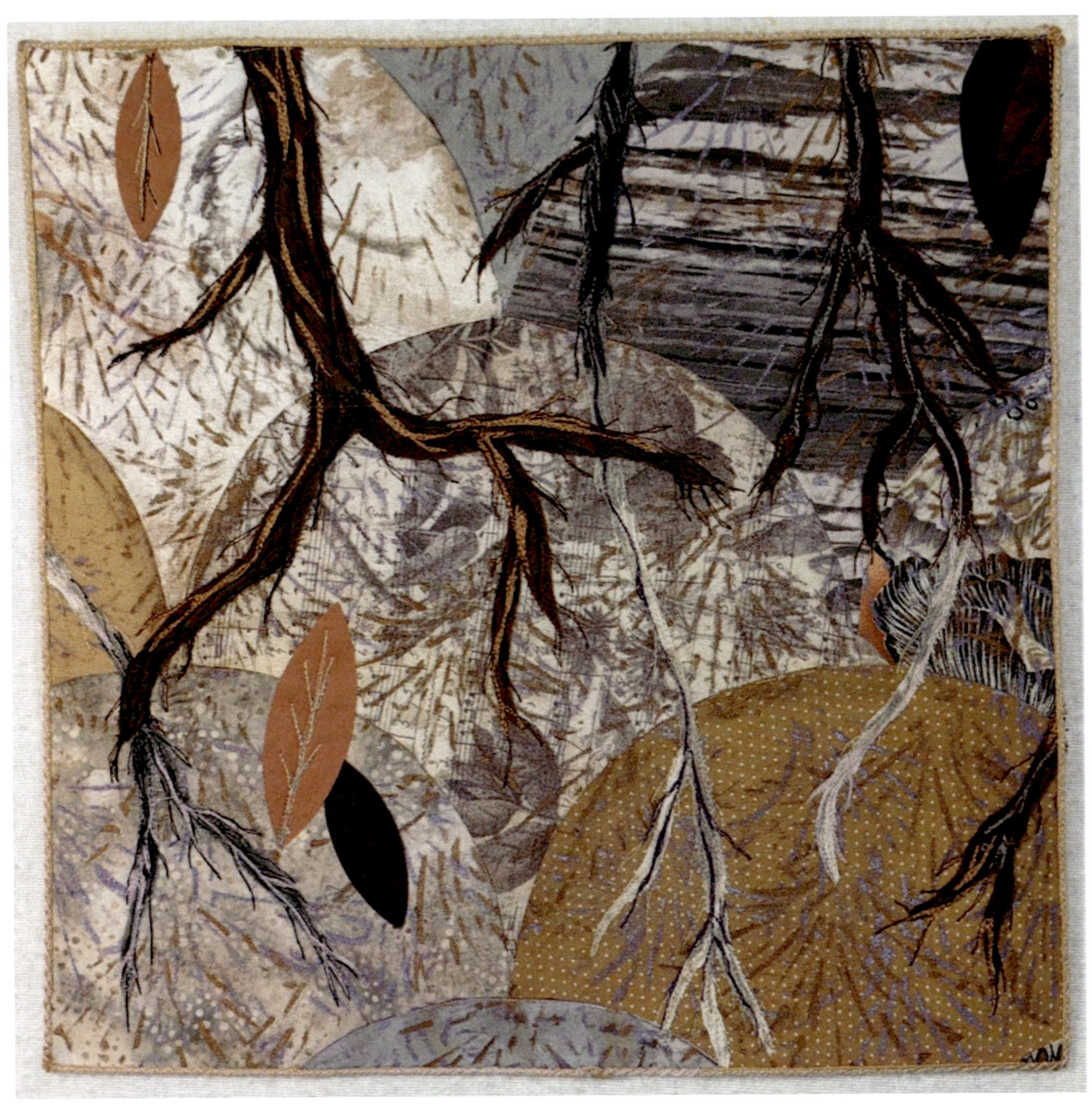

Art Quilt: "Roots VI" by Sally Harcum Maxwell

SECTION IV: UNDERGROUND, UNSEEN

Plato's Cave Redux

R. J. Keeler

Doesn't that mindless horde know it's hopeless?
They can't go back; they have seen venal Truth
and that Truth—well, it's set to set them free.
Please, stop your pitiful crawling toward that cave!

Pity, they can't bury what's been half-seen of Truth;
those shameless, unchained, multivalent lemmings
know no better life then back inside some smoky cave.
So go, new-minted Philosophers, return to ignorance;

you'll be chained again—poor imprisoned lemmings—
to unlearn that shadows on a wall are *not* a real book.
Go waddle in hot suns before slumping back to ignorance.
Fruitless! Not learn a thing you hadn't already grasped.

Against a tasty dinner you'll digest *shadow* out from *book*
and recall: all things—beans, sun—are quarried out of stars.
All awkward and alike—to darkness, you who never grasped
that punting tasty multicolors reverts you to black and white.

You retrenching Philosophers—no guidance from any star,
nor truth from any book, will henceforth set you free;
by despising the outside melting sun, you revert to b & w;
your fate is hard and sealed; escape would be quite tasteless.

Prism's Rainbow
Marjorie Gowdy

In this valley, at the lower edge of a blue misted mountain,
tumblers of gneiss and granite and quartz
heaved heavenward
before greens, before violets,
eons ago.

Volcanoes and earthquakes and storms unimaginable
rained fire from high rocky ledges
in a stream of reds and whites
from the core
of this earth.

In my hands, this clear quartz shows off her cloak
for me, her rounded edges hinting at further
beauty below. Cooled reds gyrate up from her crux,
shoot whites surface-high, and reflect in my eyes
our resting, turquoise sky.

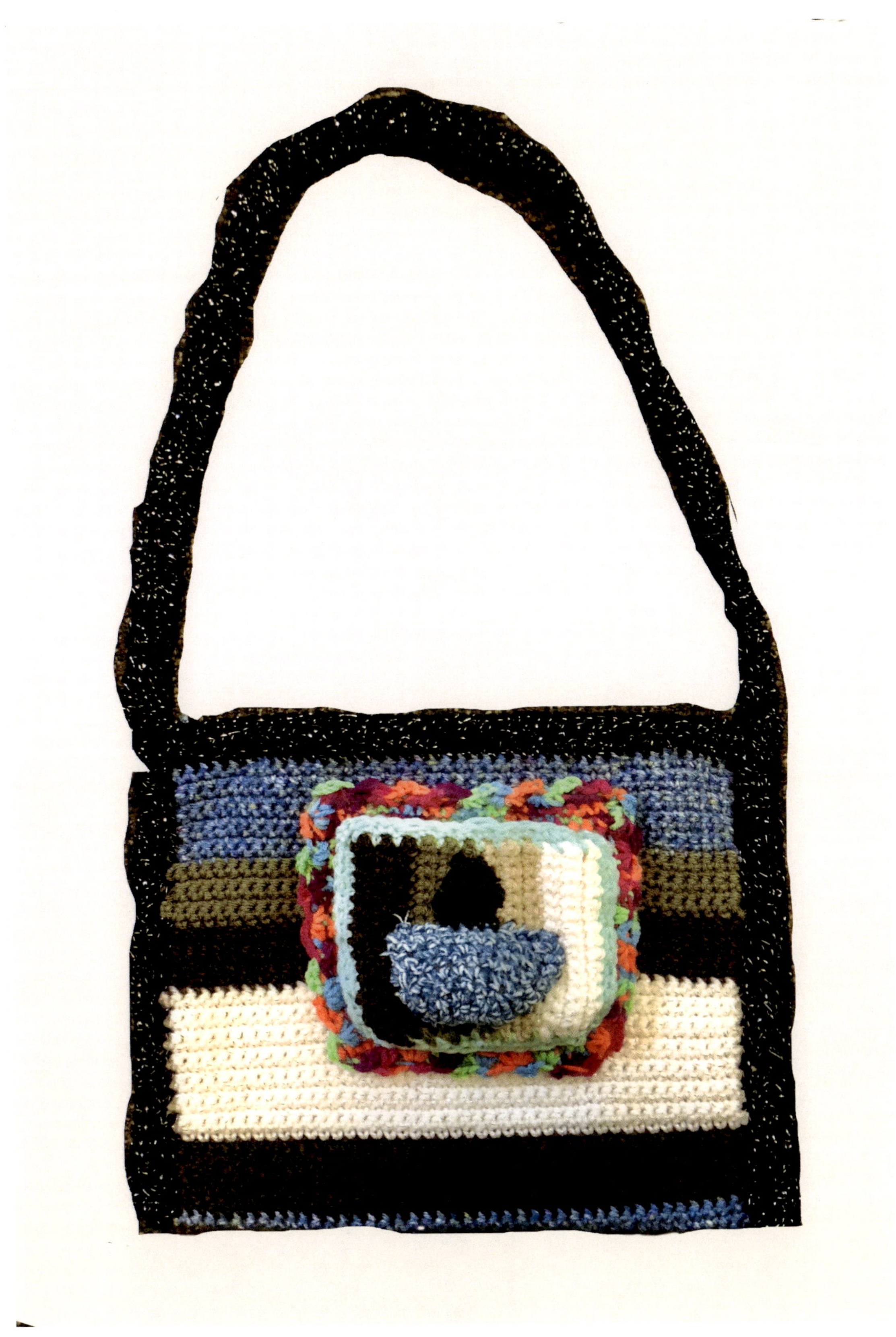

Crochet Bag : "A Bag of Geoscience" by Lauren Haygood

It All Pulses
Joan Ellen Casey

It all pulses, the whole damn thing, from the made to the unmade,
riding bits of broken star and purple cloud
humming songs of secret love out loud
leaving a trail of time.
It all pulses. The whole damn thing, from the made to the unmade,

squeezes into the forever of nothingness.
It all pulses the whole damn thing.
From the made to the unmade
dreams of God, so born to fade
into what becomes

It all pulses.
The whole damn thing, from the made to the unmade,
appears as if every part of the wave is the same
yet each dance is solo,
each move is cameo.

Something of me senses
It all pulses – the whole damn thing, from the made to the unmade,
when I drift in harmony
and know my being
as a part of being.

It all pulses, the whole damn thing, from the made to the unmade,
making me think
I am.

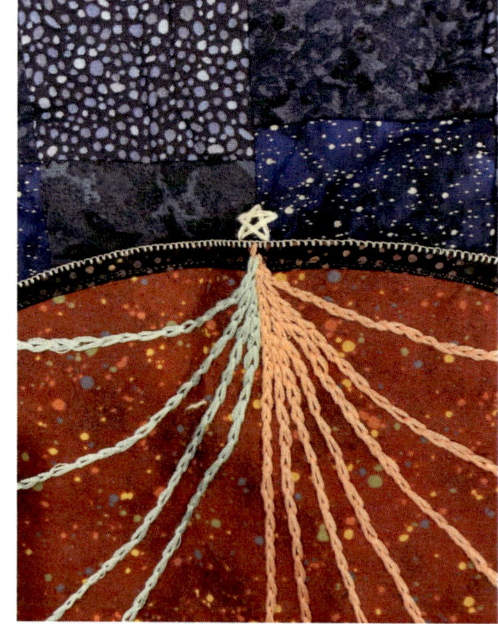

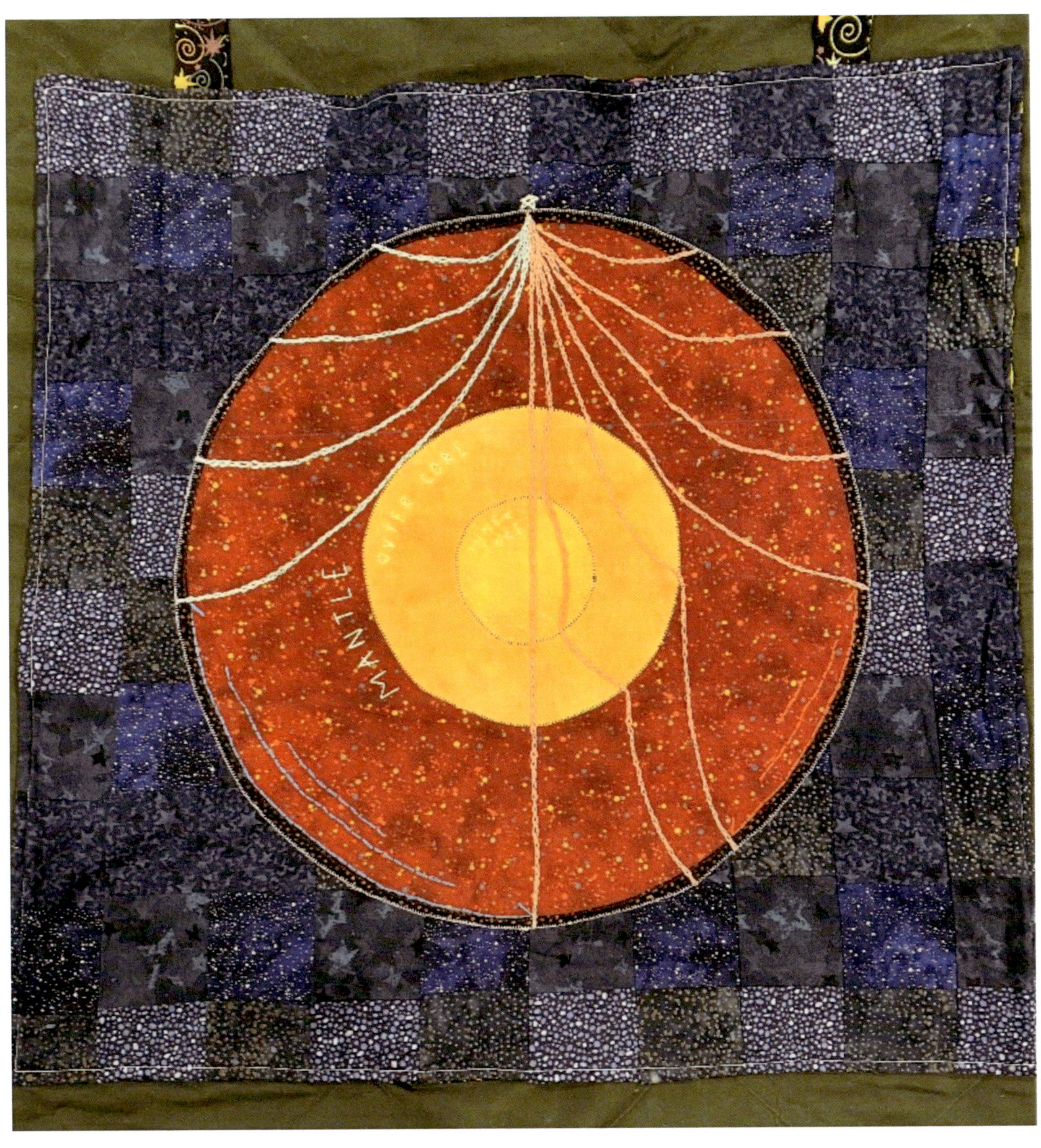

Fiber Art: "The Seismic Shadow" by Emma Burkett

Ghost Guests
Mattie Quesenberry Smith

Right here on the ridge, we cannot till three inches
Of topsoil without tipping out dead ends of limestone,
Without uncovering fossilized remnants of time spent
When water washed through the creatures of the earth
And covered House Mountain. They were: cephalopods,
Brachiopods, graptolites, and three-lobed trilobites.
The spackled tracks of these ghost guests
Chalk our garden walls, freckle rock gardens,
Splotch the new bench you built from a slab
Bursting with veins of silica and skeleton laces.
As I sit on the bench and read,
The cool and branching shades
Murmur to me folds of bifurcated time.

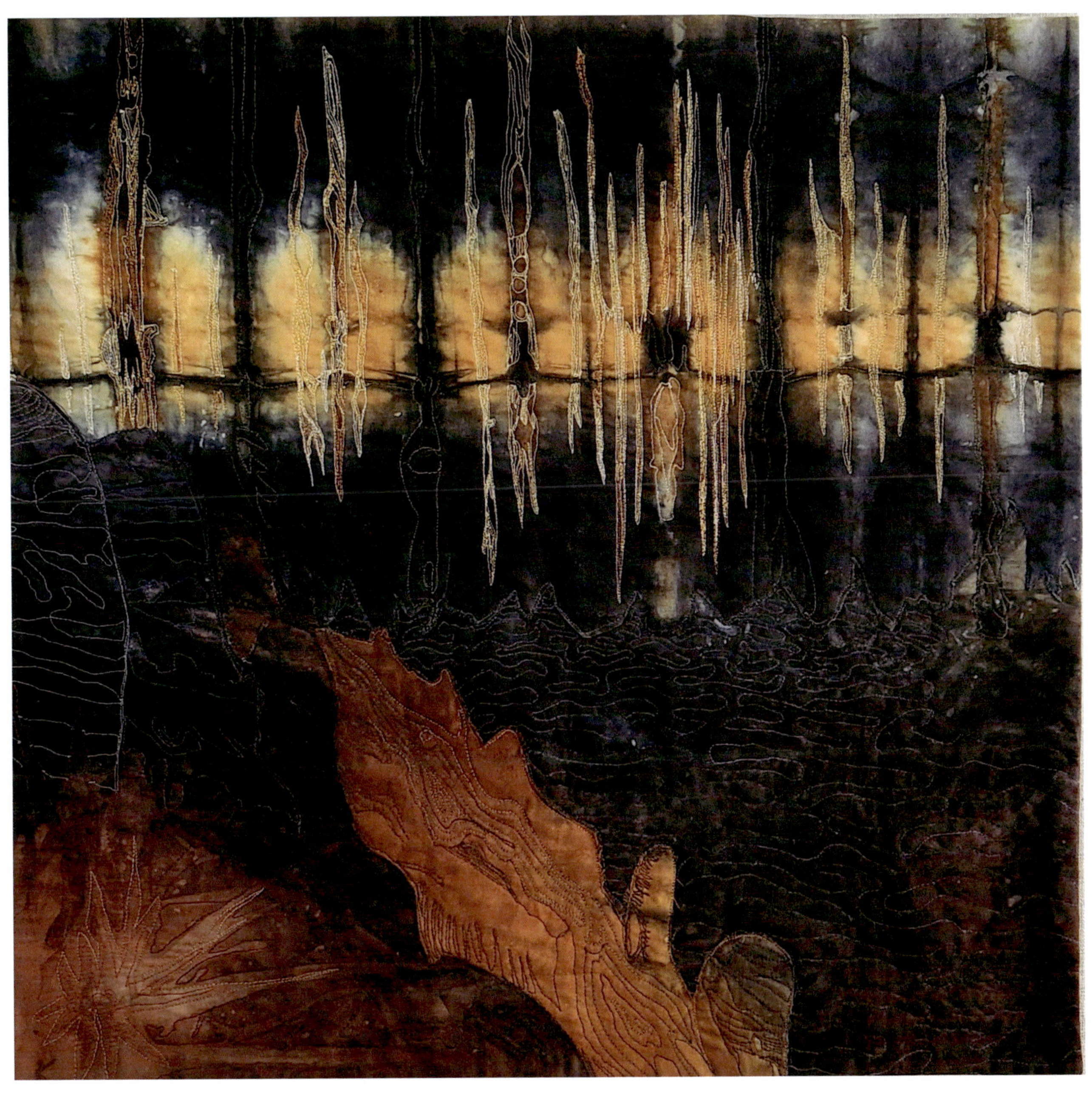

Art Quilt: "Underground Majesty" by Jody Gruendel

It's All My Fault!

Barbara M Linde

Still plates tremble, shake
Ground shudders, fissures fracture
Crust creeps, shocks, quiets

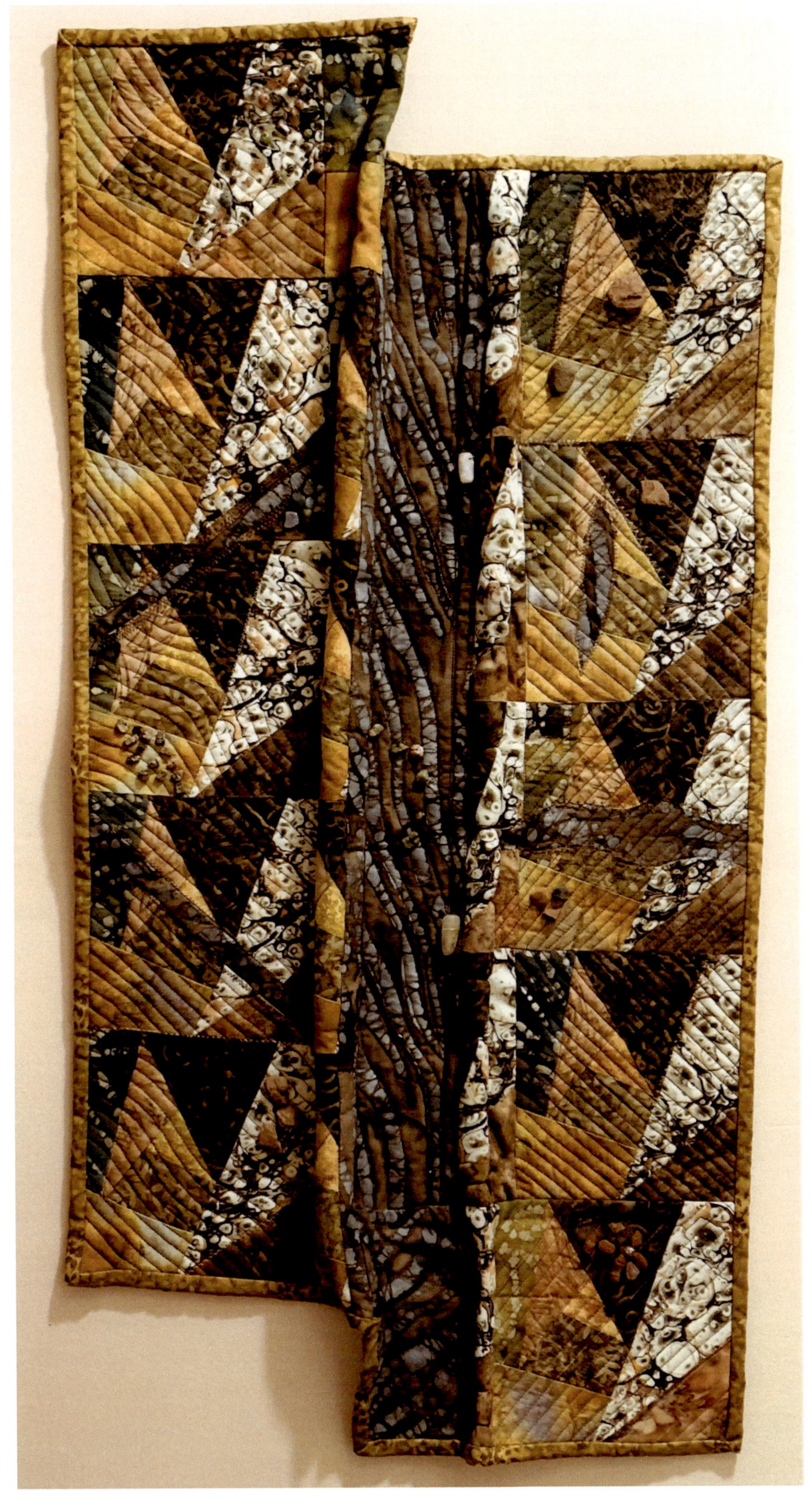

Art Quilt: “Fault” by Barbara M. Linde

Piper Jameson

Bone Deep

You feel them crawling all over you;
go to the bathroom. Wash
the feeling away, and destroy what
will sooner or later
ruin your life.
The motto to live by
is kill or be killed.
A child will wipe her
dirt-covered hands all over
the playground equipment,
the plastic slides,
the railings she's scared to
topple over.
You've scrubbed yourself clean,
whether to rid your mind of the child
you used to be
or because you're feeling
that familiar tingling in your fingers.

Sometimes it doesn't matter what you do.
They're always on you,
covering every surface and
forcing you to shake,
to cry,
to wonder if anything
was ever worth the pain.
Your hands must continuously drip
with water for eternity
because of other people's
careless filth in
the hand dryer
that threatens to infect you, too.

SECTION V: UNSEEN WITHOUT A MICROSCOPE

The Body's Hidden Lights

Chapman Hood Frazier

What is love but sparkle
    and wonder
        in the metaphysics of desire.

A feather along an inner thigh
    a breath close to the ear
        each spark
            an illumination

hidden in the heart
    synapse to synapse
        opening the mind in

a moment's instant instillation.
    Thought but a red flash in
        this universe of blue.

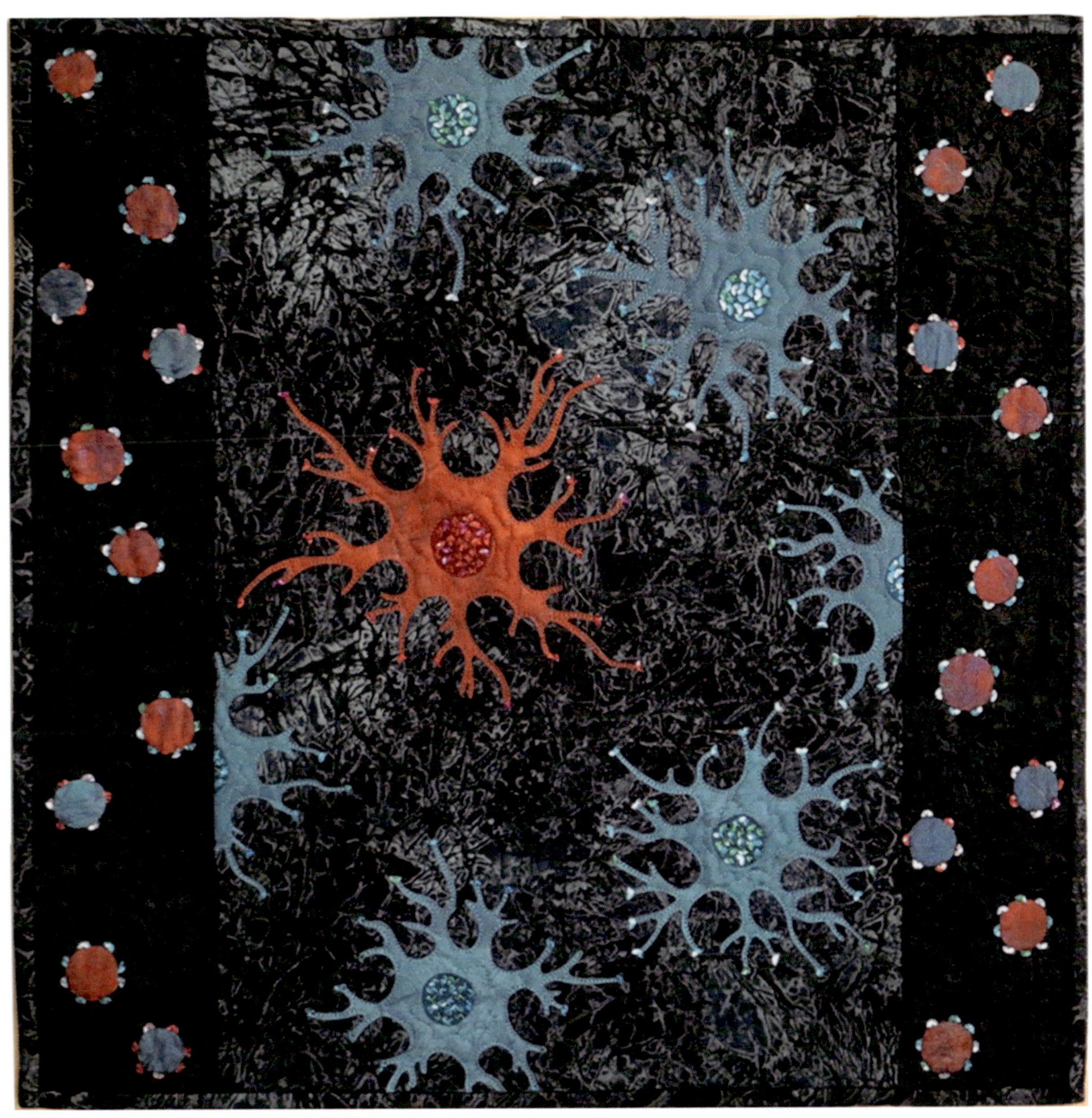

Fiber art: "Synapse" by Tricia Coulson

Endoplasmic Reticulum

Donald Beagle

At the small end of the cornucopia
You find your mirrored self strewn
Among the cells, as if the paths of life
Were endlessly forking. These selves
Within the cells are you and yet not
The you you think you know. They lie
Curled within your inner vestibules, only
To uncoil as their ribosomes release
Their tiny packets of destiny. How
Has this grown from a single cell to you
Like the homunculus whose eye sees
Through a thousand keyholes into
Your future lives? We could, of course,
Count the components of love: cisternae,
Lipids, translocons, amino acids, all aflow
Within secretory pathways that come
And go. You end where the plasma begins,
Where blood is the only truth and in
Twilight distance the Tallis choirs sing Latin
Incantations rhyming with "reticulum."

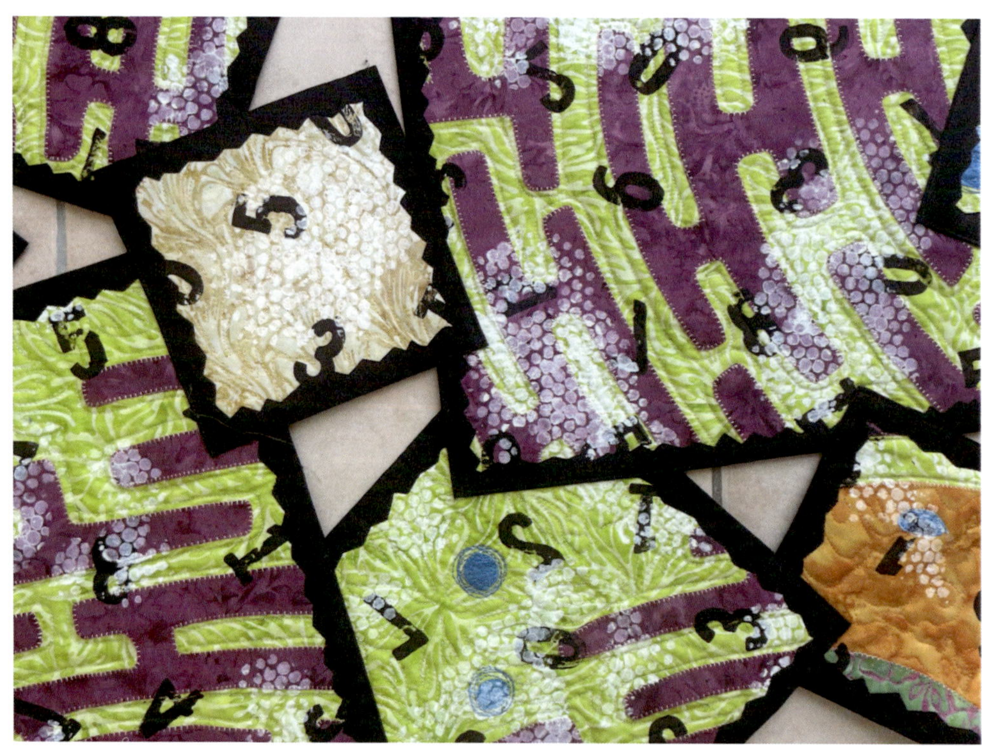

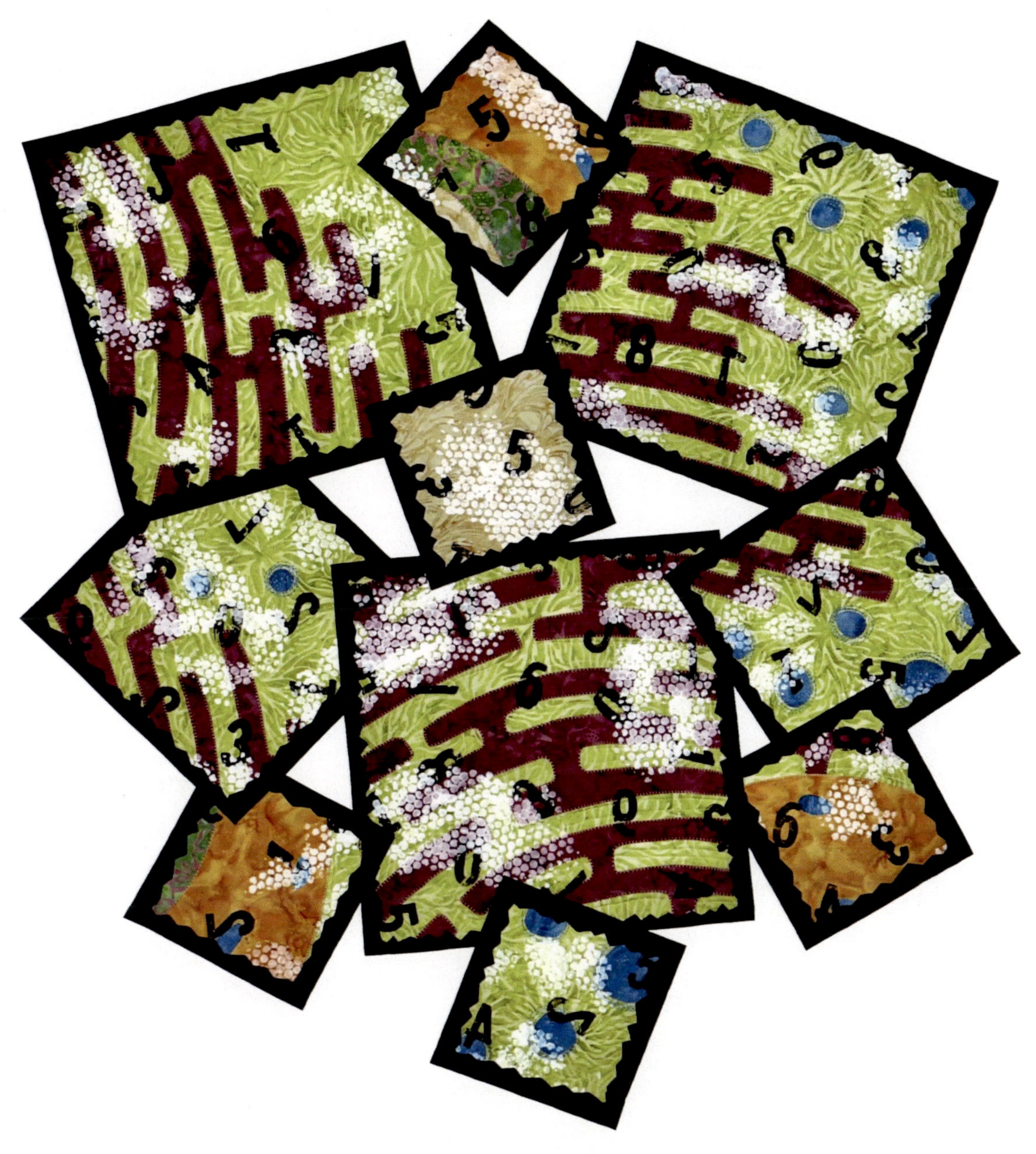

Fiber Art: Endoplasmic Reticulum" by Christie King Eckardt

H-A-B

A poem of pi (3.14159) and half-pi (1.570795)

Cathy Hailey

harmful algal blooms

losing

control of healthy waterways

poisoning

fish poisoning birds mammals humans

sunrays streaming radiance cloaking the neck body heat-glazed

transition

wavy stitches water's natural state

curvilinear ribbons layered hues lightening and darkening

~ ~ ~

to garter stitches water's warmth colors banding

nutrient beads infusing bright green roving infiltrating calm conditions

a shawl of looming toxicity

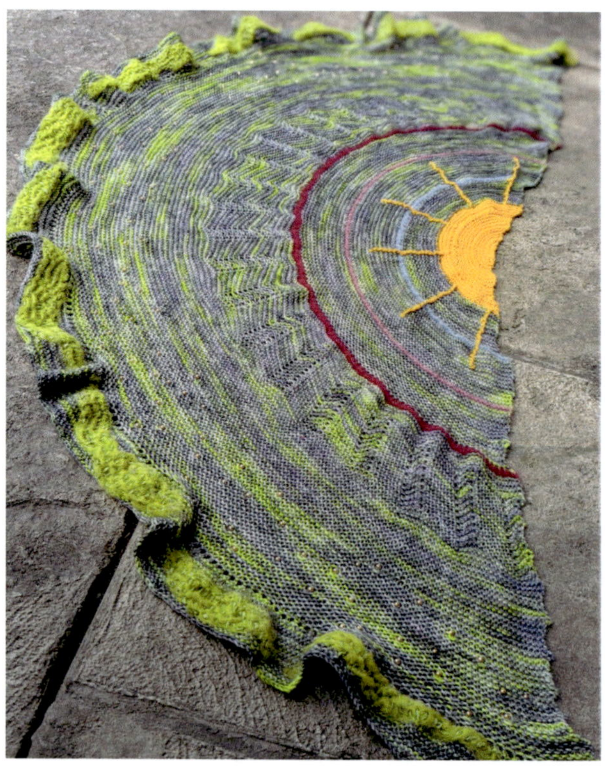

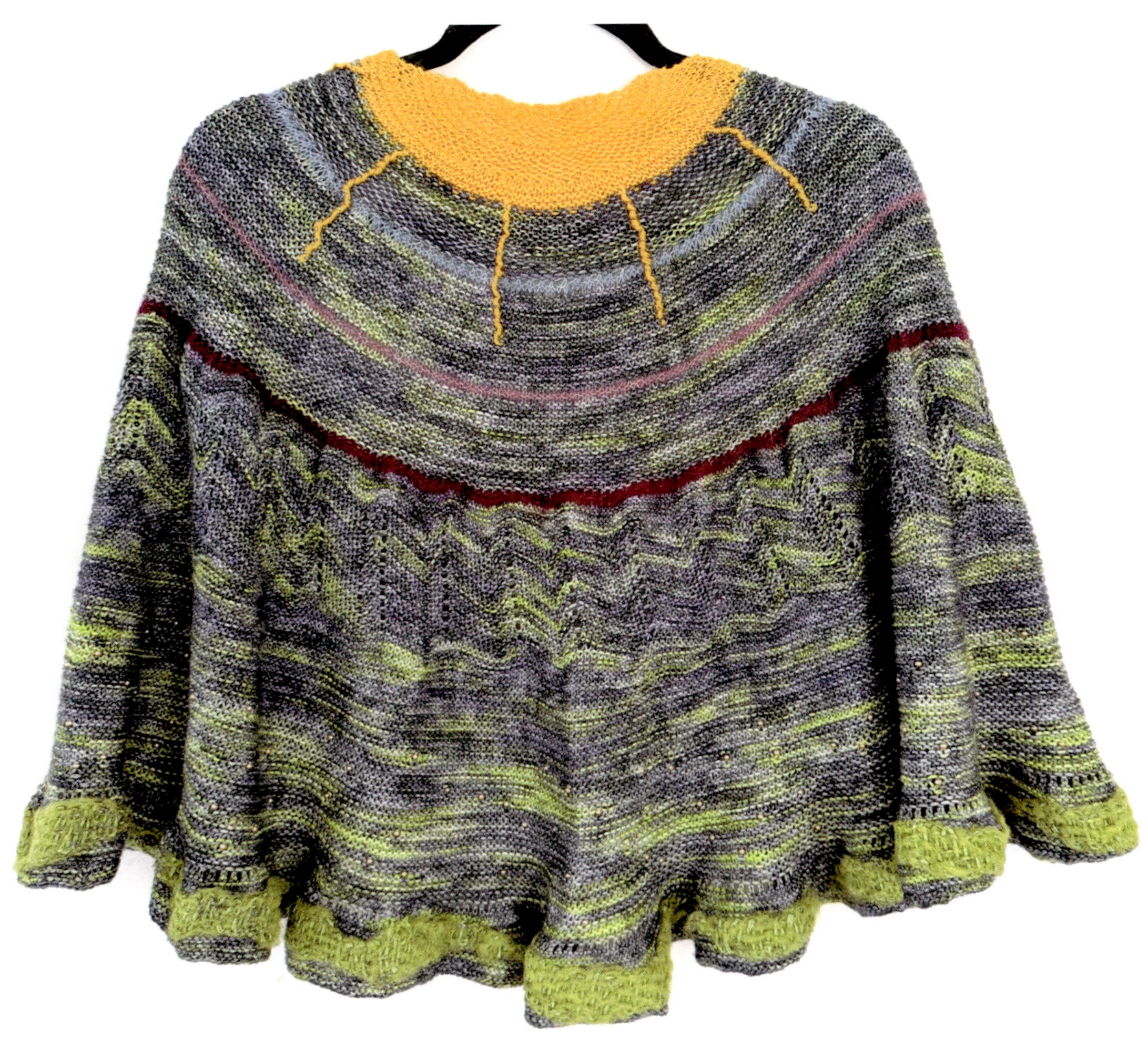

Fiber Art: "Recipe for a HAB" by Michale Glennon

The Unseen Battle

Kathleen P. Decker

inside brick hospital walls
down long corridors
behind sliding glass doors
behind an oxygen mask
deep within blood vessels
the unseen battle rages

a simple virus, studded with coat protein
ready to bind to its gigantic, languishing host
the giant's family has gathered for days, one by one in the ICU
to worry and wait, watch and wonder
will the virus win, or modern science's marvels

today is another trial-injection of new monoclonals
four antibodies, each with different epitopes
Onward with the attack on misery!

Now the COVID coat protein is surrounded with antibodies
which seek their target, glomming onto the precise spot
where the virus binds best to its host.
Breathless, for different reasons, the family and the patient,
wait and watch and wonder
For a miracle to occur!

days later, a shaky giant arises and leaves the hospital
masked, leaning on family
the pandemic turns the corner

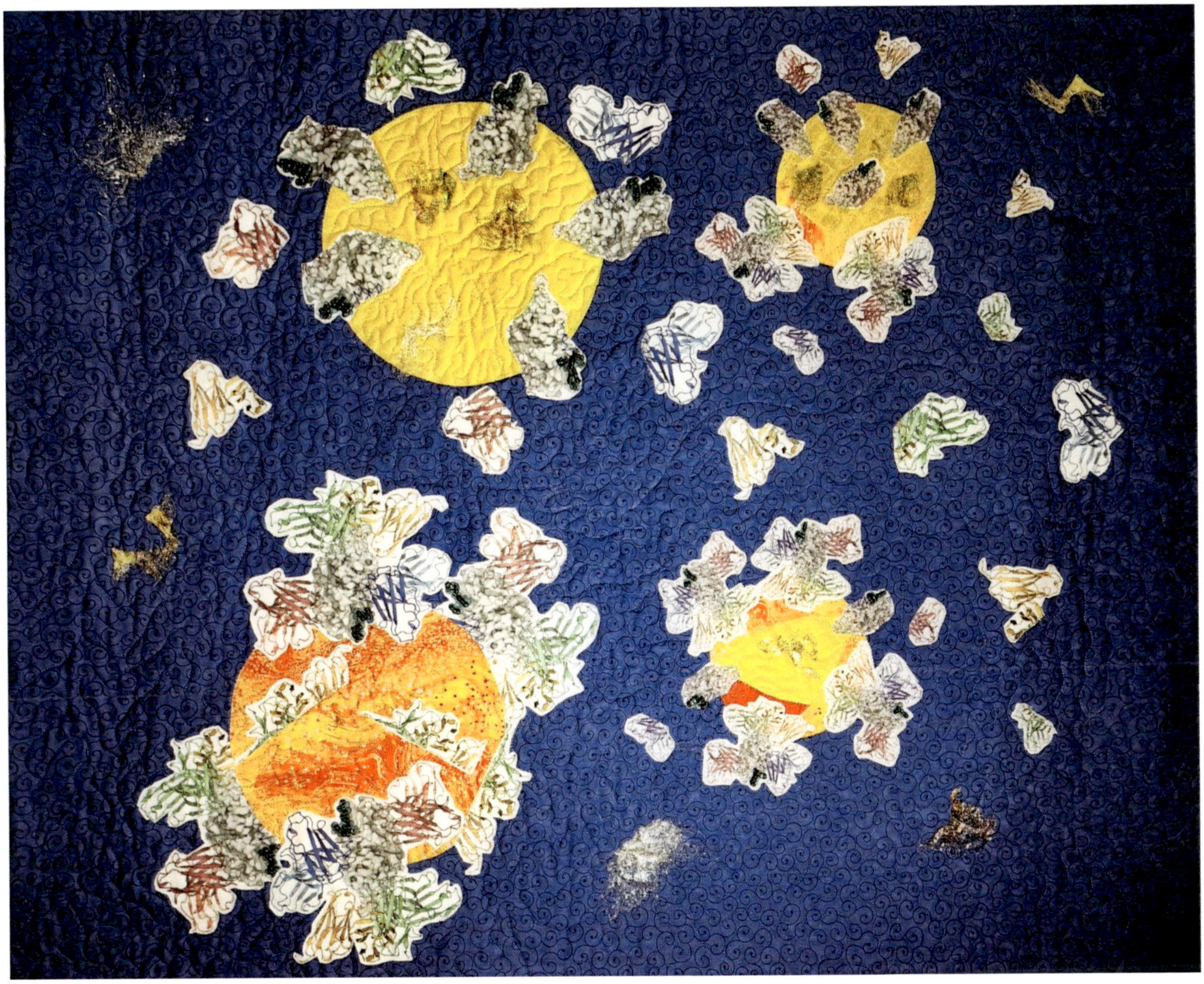

Art Quilt: "The Unseen Battle" by Kathleen P. Decker

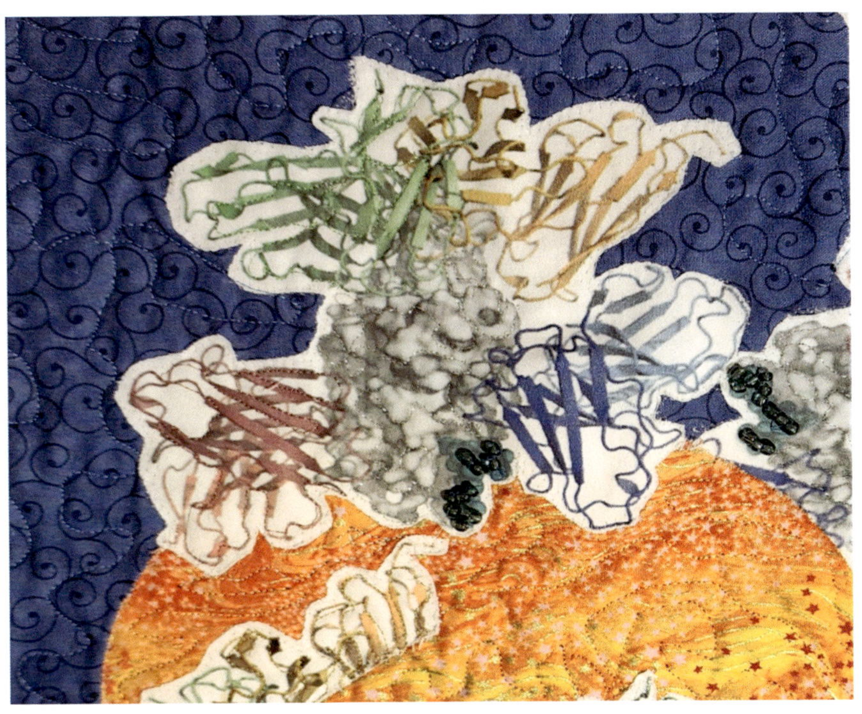

What's Seen in the Unseen

Chapman Hood Frazier

Each leaf a micro scene of itself
    in macro.

Each filament a universe
    tethered
        by an umbilicus of desire.

Each spark
    an instant   in eternities
        dark matter

This is the cosmos
    in the multiverse
        of minutiae

caught
    in a glance
        gone.

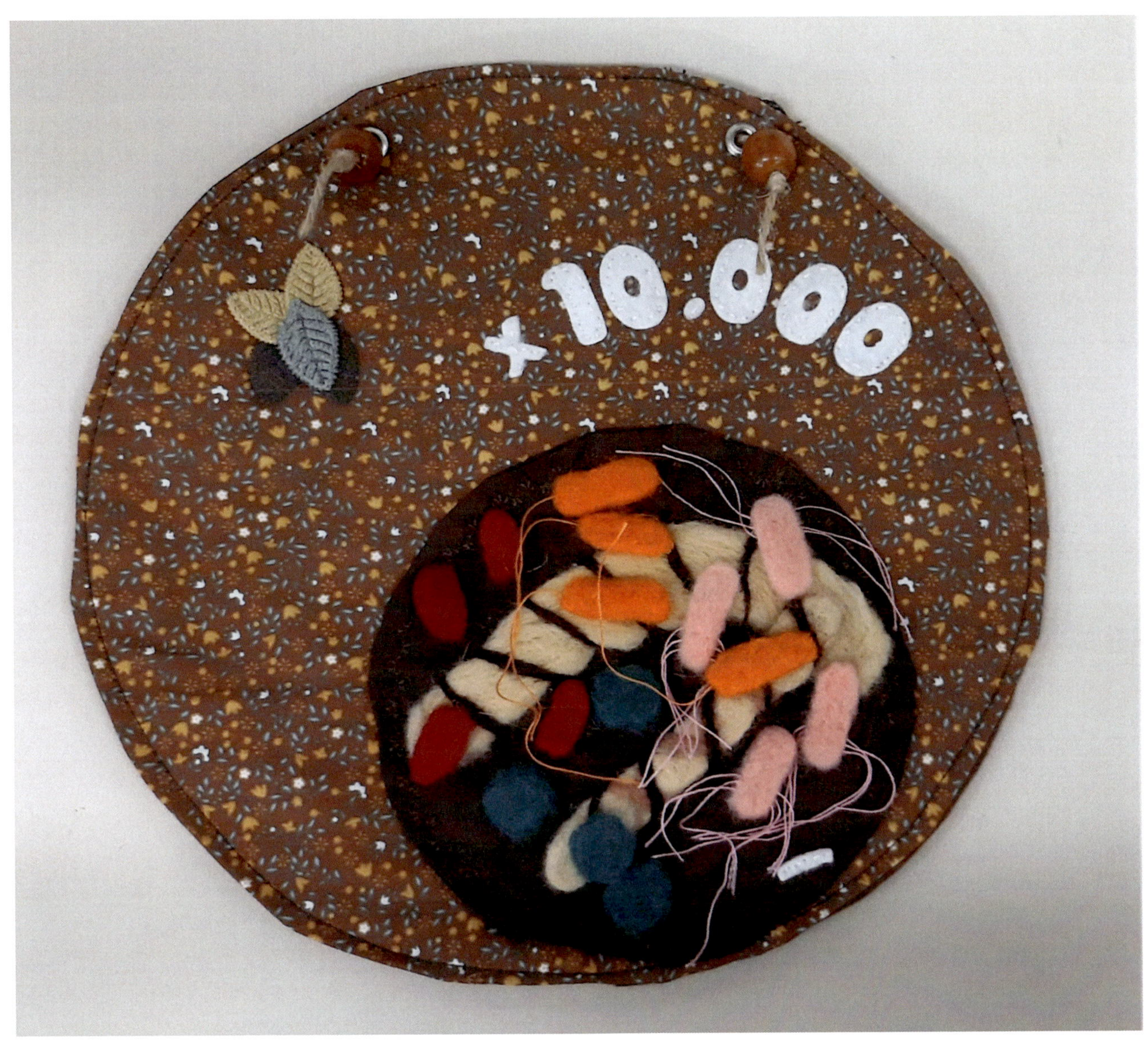

Fiber Art: "Microorganisms in action, a Microscopic View of Leaf Decomposition" by Marcela Bianchessi da Cunha-Santino

Bioremediation

Kathleen P. Decker

in the slime
in the sludge
in the sewage
where humans have left discarded
plastic bottles along with feces
a microbe mutates
to become a superhero

what if, just what if
I could eat plastic, it muses?
Of course bacteria don't muse
but if they did, that's what it thinks!
and so, chemistry takes over
Ideonella Sakaiensis begins to secrete magic PETase
and plastic bottles begin to shrivel around it

once plastic $[PET]_n$ turns to MHET,
Ideonella gobbles up MHET
and further cleaves MHET to terephalate and ethylene glycol
which as any high school chemist knows,
is food for other bugs
within six weeks, *Ideonella* eats a bottle
we thought was indestructible
Nature to our rescue, AGAIN!

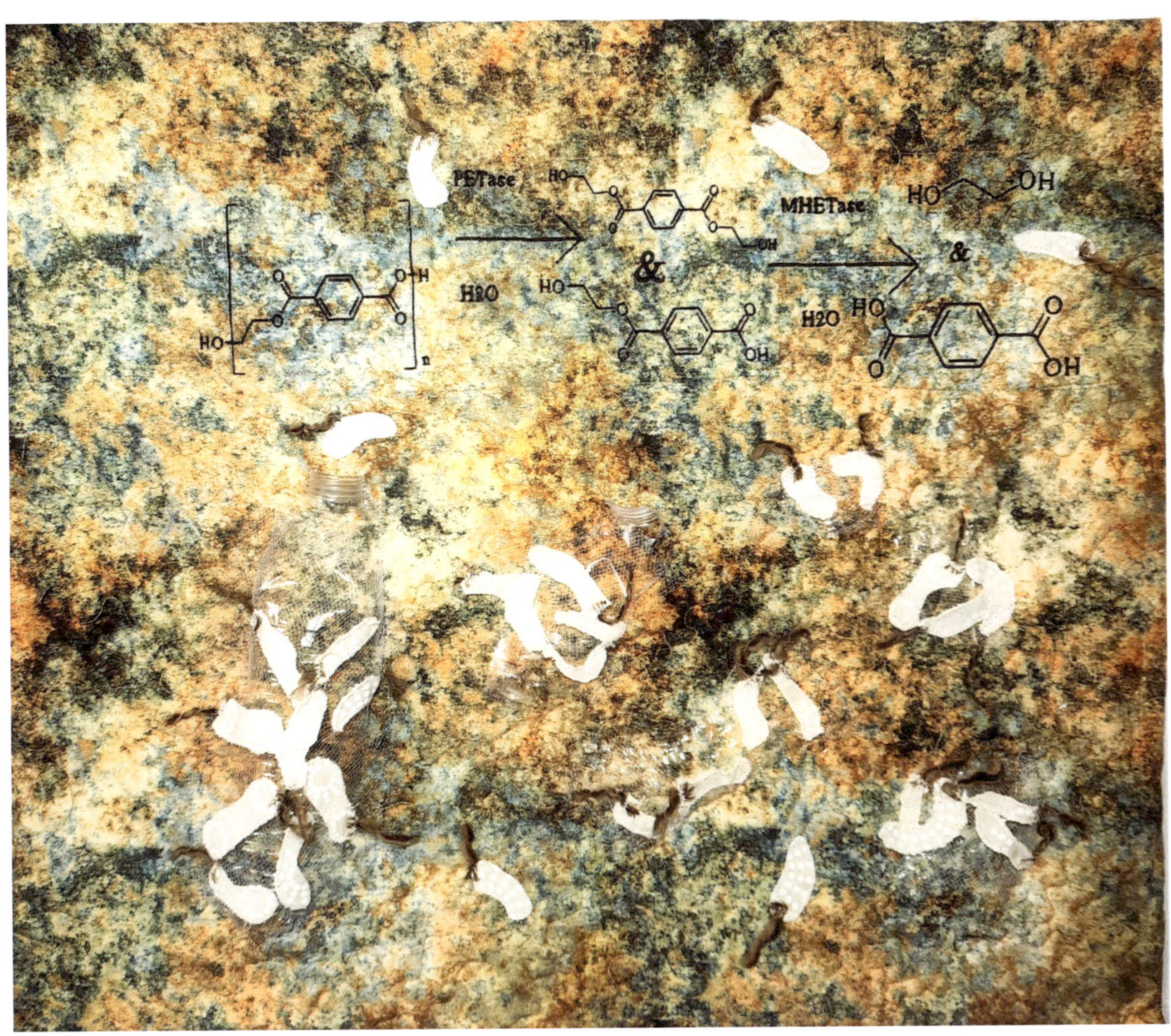

Art Quilt: “Bioremediation” by Kathleen P. Decker

SECTION VI: UNSEEN IN THE OCEAN

The Hadal* Zone

Gail Giewont

No one to row you across
the final river because it is
all water here, this lowest realm
on Earth, an underworld
of lightless pressure.

You will never see it
in your mortal life. This descent
is for scientists or movie directors
in specialized machines.

Add it to the places your ghost
will go, a bucket list for the afterlife:
there, where the weight of the ocean
rests entirely on you. Ghosts don't need
light to see, so the life that exists
where it should not is visible to you now:
hunched shrimp, sinuous eels,
thin-limbed stars, the god of death
still unseen ahead, waiting to greet you.

**the hadal zone is the deepest zone of the ocean*

To the JR

Tessa Peixoto

A ship that sailed the seven seas.
Honored by tales, images, and notes.
Adrift in blue, with not one tree,
A vessel birthed of this world's coasts.

A seafaring lab
Turned a home
where time never lags
And breaks are not postponed.

A drill that collected
Sparked such wonder and bated breath,
was never neglected
As it reached for the depths

We loved this place for all it gave,
And wait to see its sails yet wave.

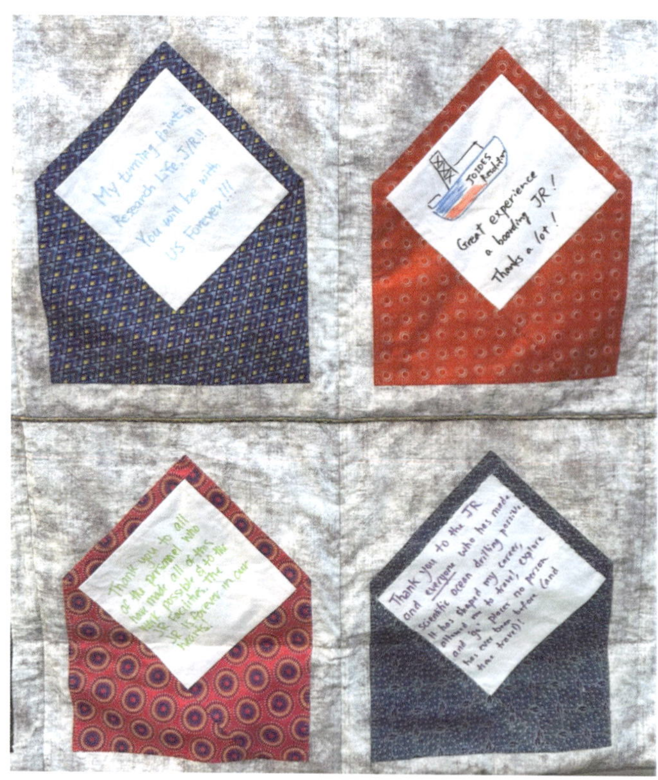

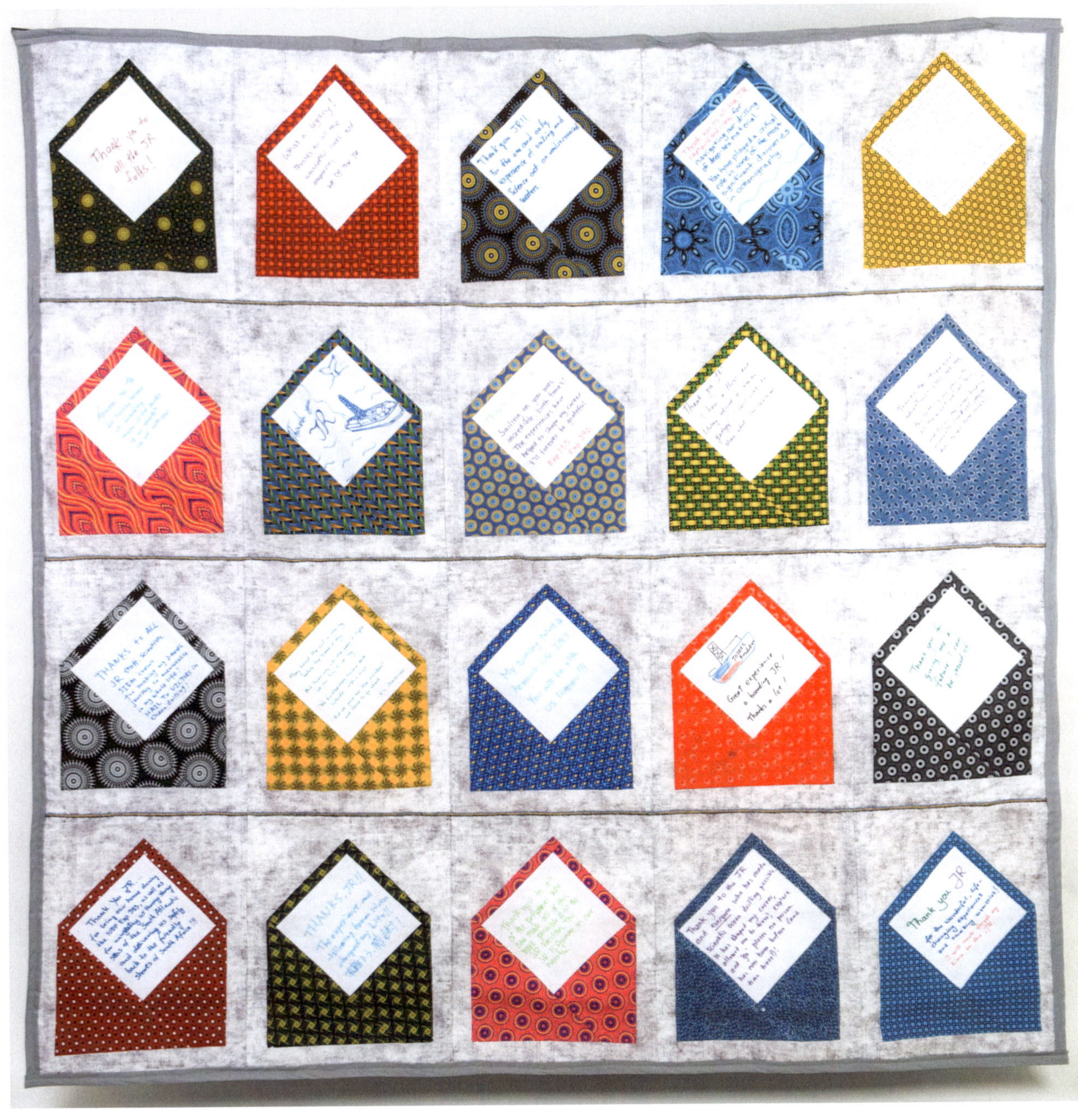

Fiber Art: "TAKK, *JOIDES Resolution* " by Laura Guertin

The Amazing Endangered Ocean

Kathleen P. Decker

if one is lucky to see
one of the three hundred or so
right whales who remain at play in the North Atlantic sea
one is fortunate indeed
or to hear humpback whales sing
when not entangled in nets and ships
beneath the surface of the ocean
as they gambol and gyre about
with other creatures as endangered as they
giant manta rays, and tiny seahorses
amidst kelp threatened by choking algae
overheated coral bleached by pollution
bluefin tuna, decimated for sushi
sea turtles, whose precarious nests are fodder for restless beachgoers toes
their diet of sea grass thinned by weeds and habitat loss
imagine oceans, barren and lifeless, with no creatures, vast soggy deserts
full of clingy algae and sandy, rocky, naked depths
What will our legacy be?
Imagine seventy-five per cent of the planet-lifeless.
Or, just maybe, we will learn in time, to keep the planet blue and thriving.

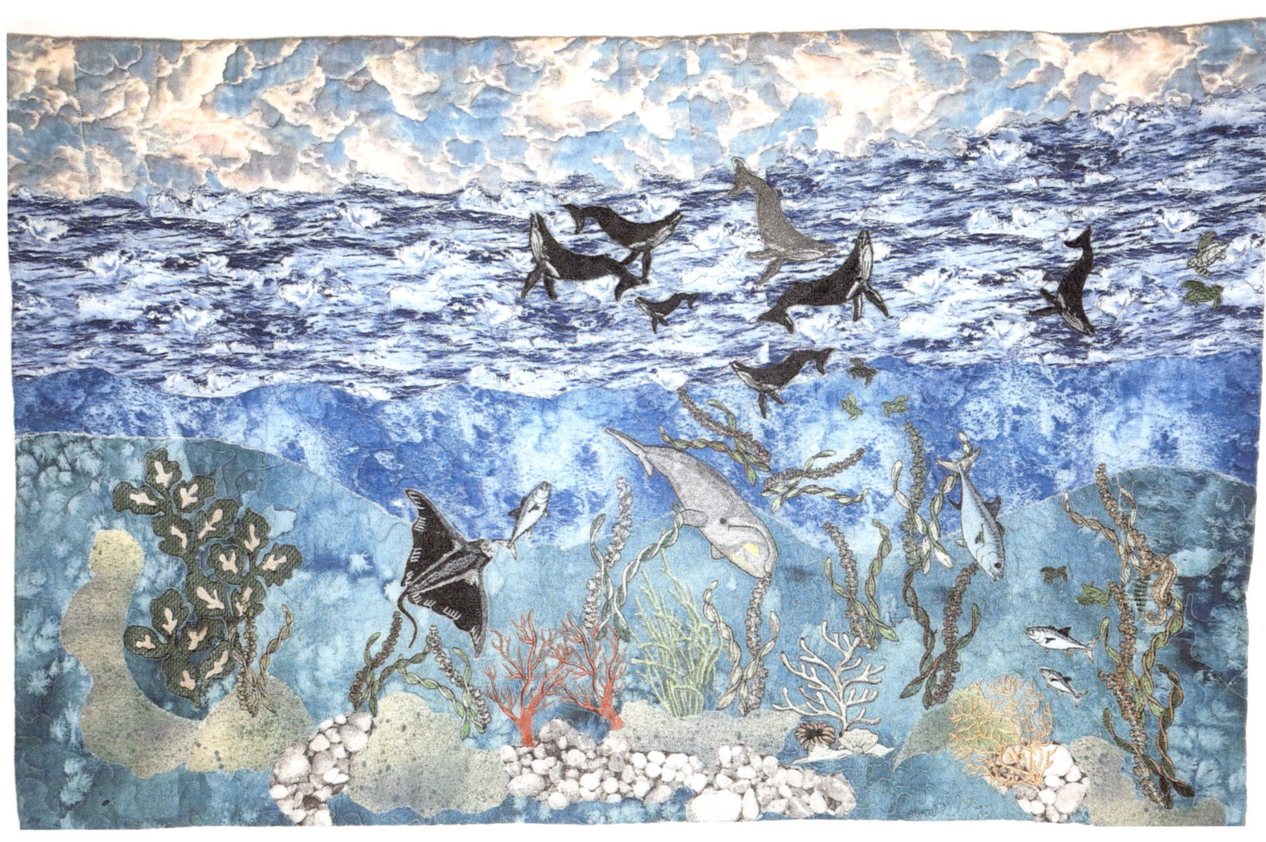

Art Quilt: "The Amazing Endangered Ocean" by Kathleen P. Decker

BLUE-GREEN ALGAE

Diana Woodcock

Way past time for me to get serious—
start practicing 'Chekhov's Gun' –
be done with leaving the rifle
hanging on the wall, if after all
is said and done, it's not going
to go off. Chekhov

got it so right. Time for me
to stop the tune short—not end
on the expected chords,
describe the cyanotoxic air I
breathe, then leave you there,
reefed in mangroves,

blessed unrest of nitrogen
and oxygen, toxin production
for three and a half billion years
in deserts, oceans, freshwater
habitats—cyanobacterial mats
resembling cracked mud,

remaining intact when touched.
Intertidal, terrestrial
communities—leave you there
with nothing but a ghutra or niqab
to filter the toxic air, and this:
True words are not beautiful,

wrote Lao Tzu. And what will you do
with Albert Schweitzer's prophecy—
man . . . will end by destroying the earth?
Yes, leave you there in the toxin-
heavy air with a prayer that you not
be separated from the source,

that you learn to *care and not care**
Cyanobacterial blooms scattering
dust across the desert's rooms.
And yet the Yellow-spotted agama
and Desert monitor** seem fine.
And the Chequered swallowtail returns

each year right on time to this
land of mist and sand scented
with Desert hyacinth. All things
terrestrial reflect nothing more
nor less than the celestial,
even noxious blue-green algae.

Like Tiffany's technique of favrile,
these surreal mats shift in light—
morning, noon, night—
a pale pewter opalescence,
I should stop right here,
let you fear what happens next

as you hold one intact mat

in your palm and breathe

in the lethal desert breeze,

not mention the connection

to Lake Michigan and Lake

Champlain, let this be the end.

*T.S. Eliot, ** Least Concern (LC) on the IUCN Red List

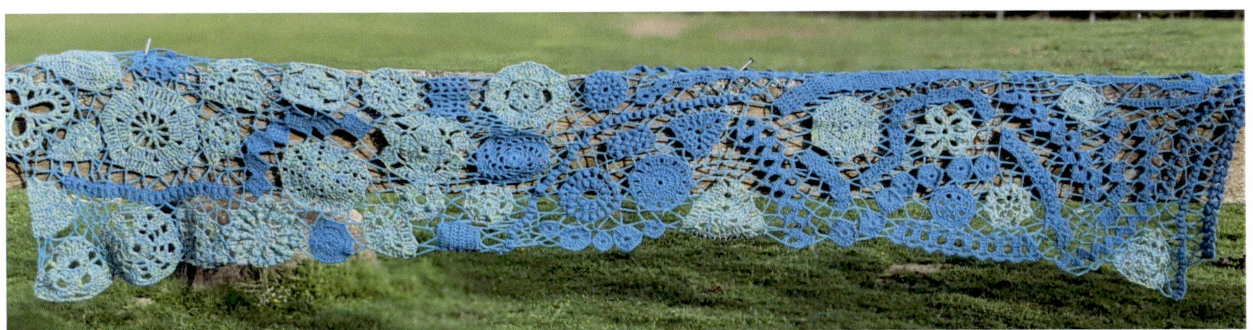

Fiber Art: “Plankton” by Michale Glennon

Prying into the Past We Left Behind
Alicia Swain

When our bodies wandered from the depths of the sea
to the sand along its shores, we forsook the companions
we floated beside—friendships built in a shared domain.
When our spines lifted, reached toward the sun,
we abandoned our understanding of jellyfish,
of invertebrates that wander the ocean and hover
along its floor. When we chose grassy land, we surrendered
our right to comprehend the sensation of wriggling
bulbous bodies through a world of brine, yet our memories
cannot conjure our history, and our minds urge us to capture
the life we left behind into nylon and polyester—
just so we can observe and exploit the families
and the sunken world we chose to leave behind.

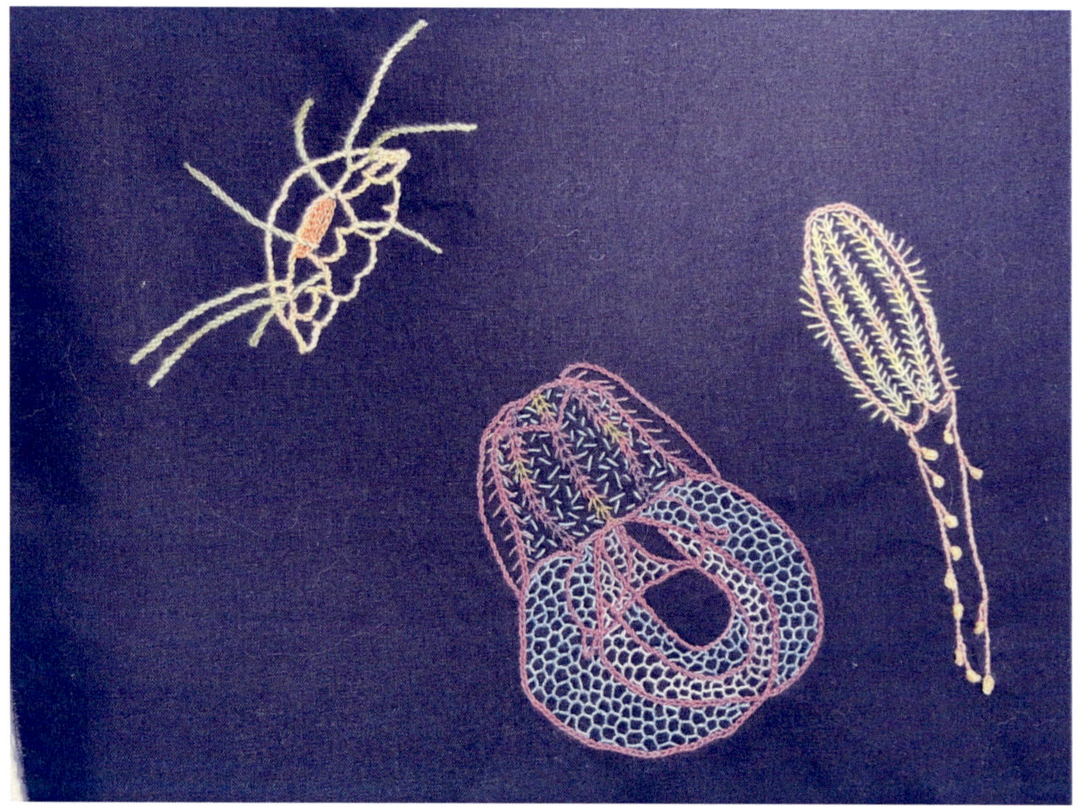

Fiber Art: "Gelatinous Zooplankton" by Kate Hedstrom

Fiber Art: "Gelatinous Zooplankton" by Kate Hedstrom

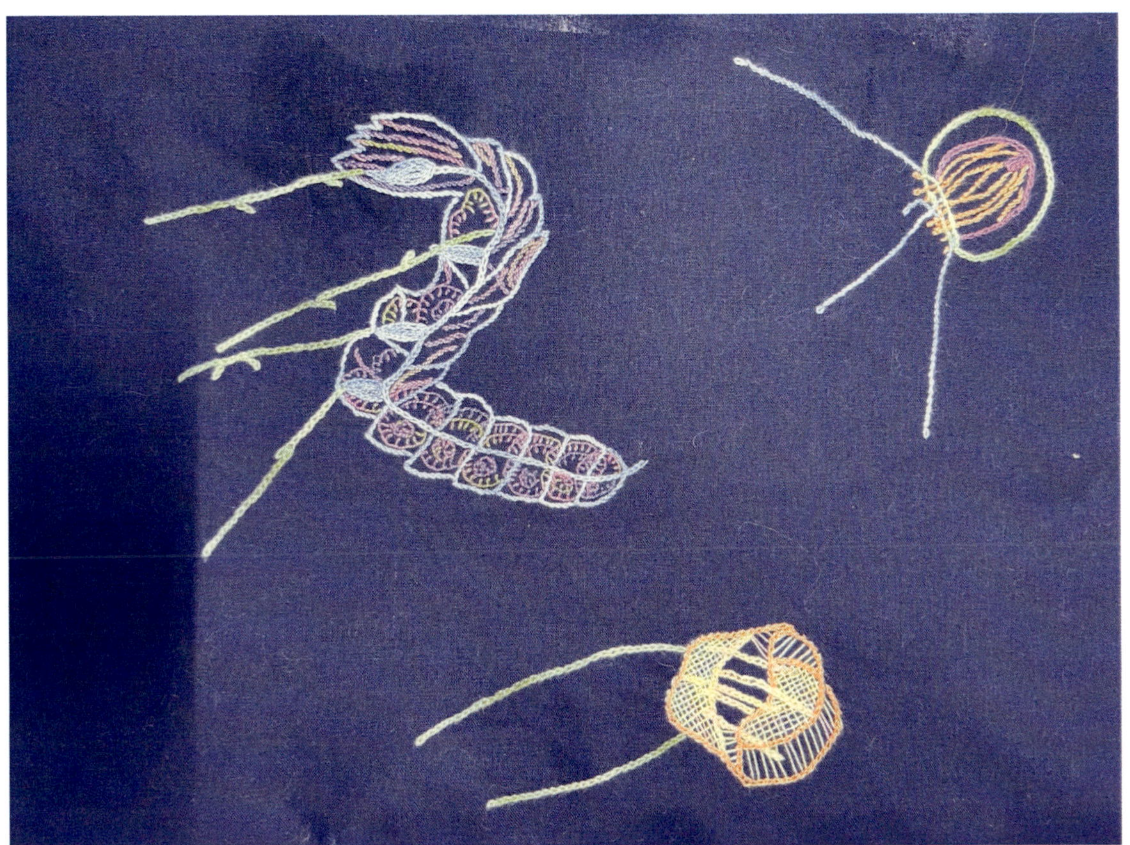

The Plankton Crisis

Emily Bilman

Like a tattered tartan, the algae-
weft gnaws the lacustrine warp
suffocating the bluegill, bass, and trout –
the phosphorus fraught waters eaten
by parasite-toxins might ultimately paralyze
the Coriolis currents that clear
our air with wind, cloud, and rain,
our life-sustaining looms.

on gelatinous zooplankton as viewed through the ISIIS deep-focus particle imager

Jae Dyche

uncountable not
as in countless, but rather
as in unable to be
counted, fragile, soft bodies–
some no more than yawning O's or

Lilliputian
bells, flickering cilia
in sun-starved darkness–
simply too delicate for
marine researchers to grasp

an exact count,
yet hypothesize some-
thing like two-hundred
trillion petagrams of
gelatinous zooplankton,

the same weight as
one teaspoon of neutron star
or the world's crude oil
production in two-thousand-
nine; off the coast of Western

Australia, a
three hundred ninety
foot siphonophore
colony spirals as if
a small galaxy in blue

open waters, perhaps
the longest animal to
have ever existed,
exceeding the longest blue
whale by far, yet somehow it

wasn't discovered
until two-thousand-twenty
while the earliest
fossils of gelatinous
plankton date back to the late

Cambrian, five-
hundred million years ago
when the infant Earth
was nothing but an endless
stretch of sea teaming

with a microscopic
cosmos of comb jellies,
salphs and medusea
and chaetognaths adrift in
waters without time, creatures

at once seemingly
insignificant
and as infinite as the
grains of matter meandering
through the deep universe.

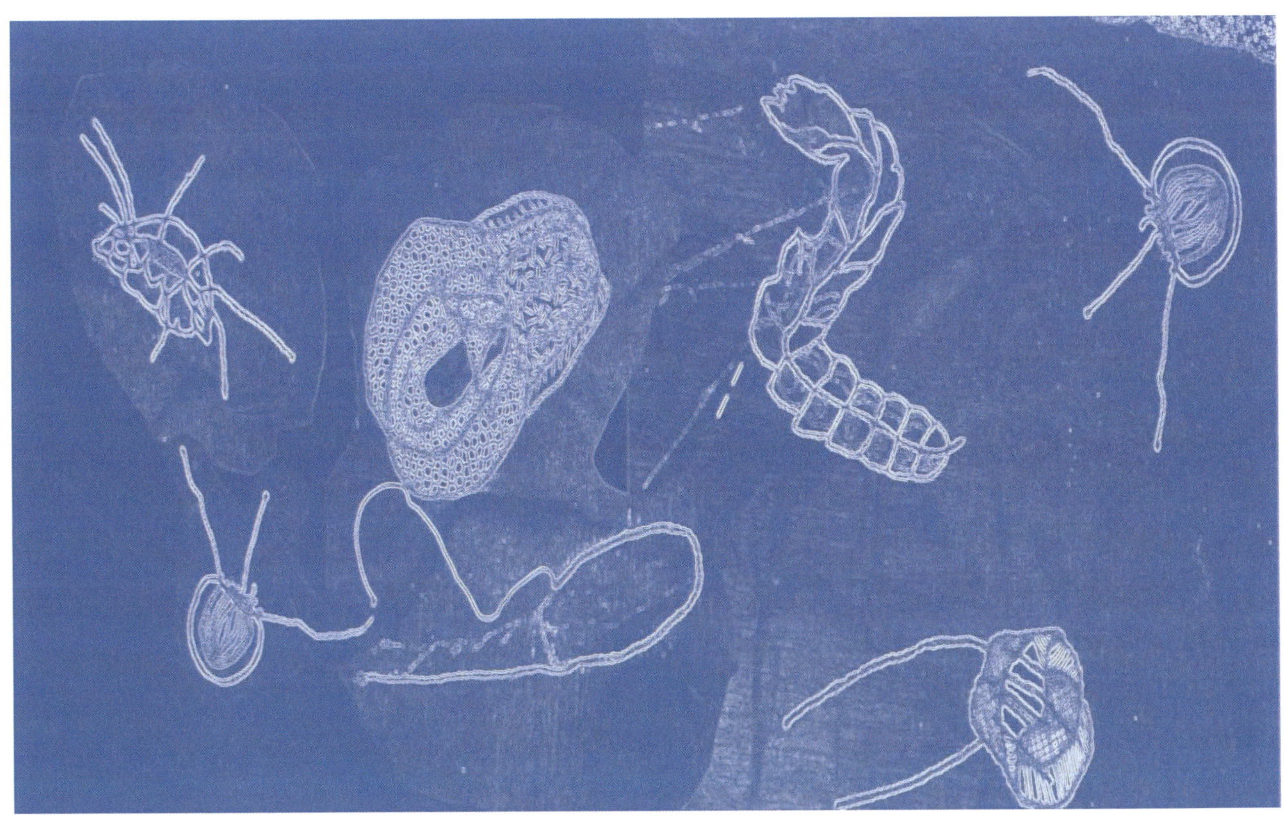

Fiber art/Graphic Art: "Gelatinous Zooplankton" by Kate Hedstrom/Kathleen P. Decker

Maintaining Ship Position At Sea
Laura Guertin

How does a ship stay in place
while drilling deep sea
sediment and ocean crust?

Dynamic Positioning
holds the location
above the reentry cone.

This technology allows
a ship to not have
to drop anchor for coring.

The *JOIDES Resolution*
has six thruster pairs
in their retractable pods

and are raised during transit.
The pods are lowered
once the JR is on site.

The ship's two main propellers
way back at the stern
also keep the ship in place.

Once stationary, science
activities start,
with safety prioritized.

The JR may look stopped, still.
But all the movement
is now on the drilling deck.

Scientists eagerly and
anxiously await
samples up from the deep sea.

Dynamic Positioning,
oceanographers
value your technology.

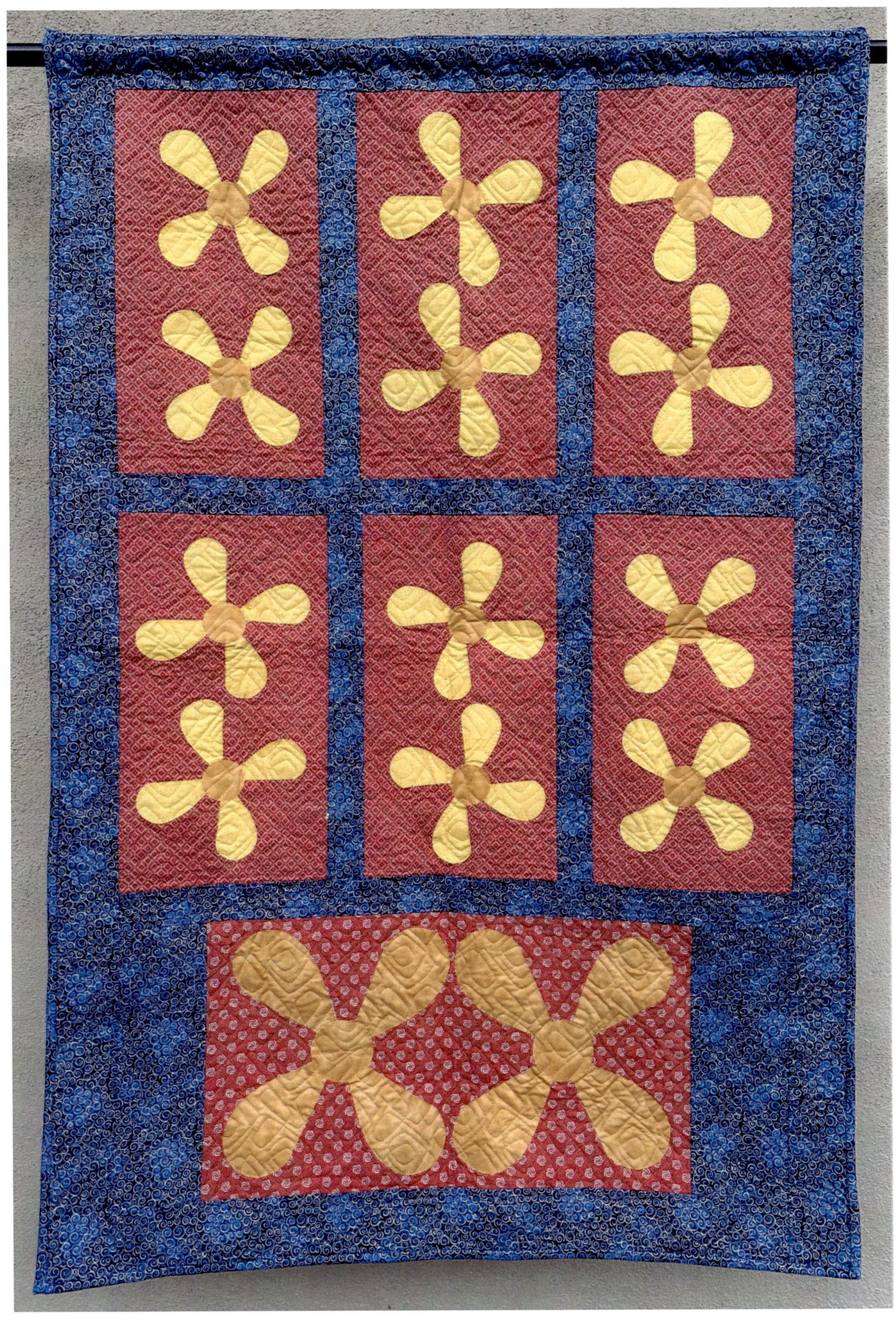

Fiber Art: "DPS Got to Go Round" by Laura Guertin

Searching Secret

Wayne David Hubbard

ocean core hidden
deep clues within earth's stitches
the impact, preserved

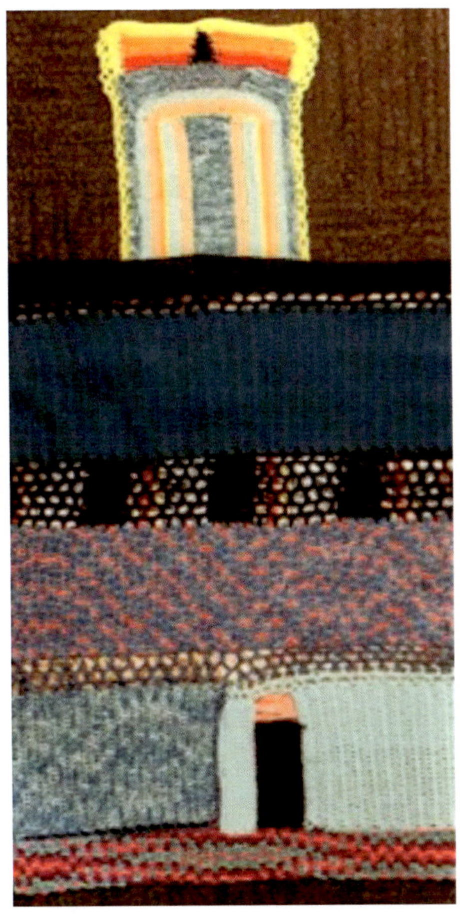

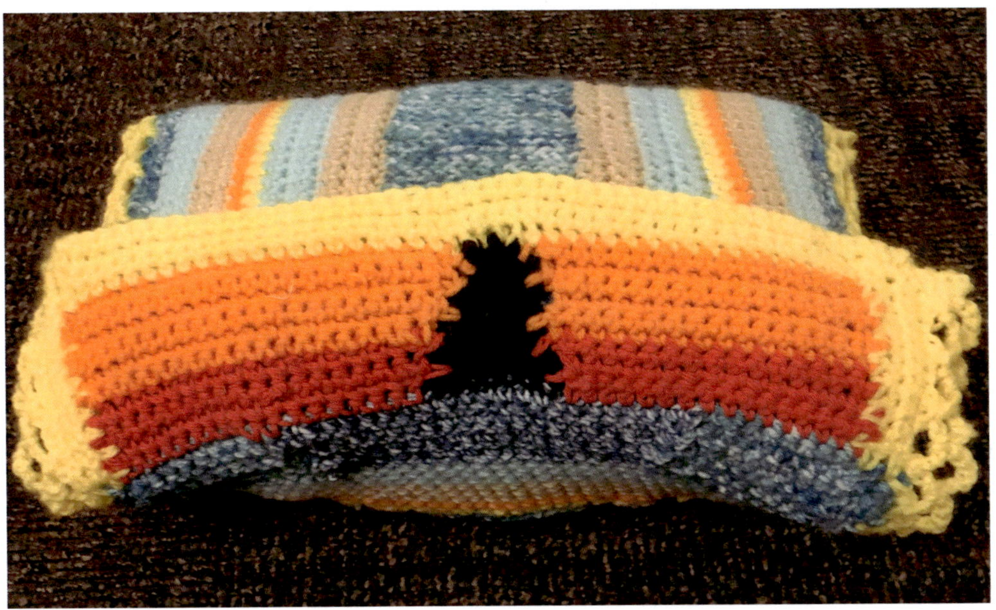

Fiber Art: "Searching for Earth's Secrets: Hidden Impacts of Deep-Sea Sediments" by Lauren Haygood

ARTIST/POET/SCIENTIST BIOS:

Donald Beagle's poetry has appeared in journals, anthologies, and 5 published collections. During his graduate work at the University of Michigan, his first collection won the top prize in the annual Hopwood Awards. By the late 1980's he was teaching Evening Poetry Workshops at Duke University. Readers can browse his author page for interviews, published reviews, and podcast readings: donaldbeagle.carrd.co

Dr. Emily Bilman is a widely published and anthologized author of poetry, literary essays, and short stories. Her PhD dissertation, *The Psychodynamics of Poetry,* was published by Lambert Academic in 2010. Slatkine S.A. published *La rivière de soi* (2010) in Geneva. *Modern Ekphrasis* (2013) was published by Peter Lang Academic, CH. Her poetry books, *A Woman by A Well* (2015), *Resilience* (2015), *The Threshold of Broken Waters* (2018), *Apperception* (2020), and *The Undertow* (2023) were all published by Matador Books UK that just published a new version of *Resilience* (2025). Her sonnet, "Pathfinder" was planted on the moon's southern pole by a time-capsule in 2024. She blogs on http://www.emiliebilman.wix.com/emily-bilman

Joyce Brinkman: Indiana Poet Laureate 2002-2008, believes in poetry as public art. She creates public poetry projects involving her poems and the poems of others. She thinks she would be frightened by dinosaurs, but otherwise, loves all the wild, living things on Earth. She knows weeds are simply plants humans haven't discovered how to use. Joyce loves to collaborate. She and Dr. Foronda have been collaborating for over a decade. Joyce was lead editor of *The Polaris Trilogy*, a world anthology on its way to the Moon via a NASA flight to be part of the Lunar Codex for millions of years. Other publications include *Seasons of Sharing: A Kasen Renku Collaboration, Catena Poetica: An International Collaboration,* and *Elizabeth Barrett Browning* in the Literary Portals to Prayer Series. Joyce has received fellowships from the Mary Anderson Center for the Arts, the Vermont Studio, and the Indianapolis Arts Council.

Sarah-Beth Bradley is a science communicator in Galway, Ireland. She started knitting in 2020 when she ran out of distractions from her undergraduate thesis. She is very passionate about the value of creativity in science. She can often be found knitting or out looking for bats. Her blog can be found at https://artesetnaturam.home.blog/

Megan Brown is a senior research associate in medical education at Newcastle University in the UK. She initially trained as a doctor, before leaving to pursue a PhD in educational research. She is dedicated to researching education and training for health professionals, and advocating for changes that improve professionals' and patients' experiences. She is multiply disabled and Autistic. Poetry has always been a way for her to process, reflect, and communicate experiences that she finds difficult to express through more conventional or neurotypical forms of communication.

Emma M. Burkett is a PhD candidate at the University of New Hampshire studying how magma moves and is stored in volcanoes before eruptions. She connects geochemistry to surficial unrest through remote sensing and diffusion chronometry, with a passion for understanding magma dynamics and volcanic hazards. She also finds joy in "granny hobbies" like knitting, beading, embroidery, crocheting and quilting, which connect her to grandmother and honor generational creativity. Blending science and art, she uses textile crafts as an accessible, engaging way to share volcano science in a non-threatening way, making complex geologic processes more approachable through handmade artistry.

ARTIST/POET/SCIENTIST BIOS cont'd.:

Samantha Carr is based in Plymouth where she is a Ph.D. Creative Writing candidate exploring chronic illness through prose poetry. Her work has been published in Acumen, Arc, Corporeal, Consilience and The Storms Journal. She can be found on Threads and Instagram as @samc4_rr.

Joan Ellen Casey has written poetry since she was twelve years old, but never went public until 2011. Since then, she has won awards and appeared in many anthologies. Her writing is influenced by her life's roles, an insatiable curiosity, a doctorate degree, and trekking alone through twenty-three countries. She writes to share her experiences.

Loralee Clark resides in Virginia. Her website is sites.google.com/view/loraleeclark. She has a book in press, "Solemnity Rites" (Prolific Pulse Press, LLC) and has been published recently in Periwinkle Pelican, White Stag Journal, Chewers by Masticadores, Nude Bruce Review, Lucky Leaves, Everscribe, The Rockford Review, and Soul Poetry, Prose and Art Magazine.

Tricia Coulson lives in Minnesota on a lake with her husband. There she works part-time in her loft studio. She graduated with a degree in art with an emphasis in textile design and has been creating art for thirty years. Tricia works with several art clubs and exhibits with one of them every year. She also exhibits regionally as well as nationally. Her goal is to exhibit in every state. So far she has made it to 37 states.

Marcela Bianchessi da Cunha-Santino is an associate professor at the Universidad Federal de São Carlos in Brazil. She devotes her career to teaching environmental sciences disciplines. She creates content-based instructional materials to engage lecture and laboratory students in critical thinking and investigative practices. Her research focuses on Aquatic Sciences, and she is passionate about aquatic plants. Sewing has always been a part of her life. When she was little, she would sleep in her grandmother's scrap box. For her, textile arts are a therapeutic hobby!

Dr. Kathleen P. Decker is a retired psychiatrist and molecular neurobiologist. She is Past President of the National League of American Pen Women, Seattle Branch, and is President of the Poetry Society of Virginia. Her poetry include *Russian Reverie, Whispers on Paper, Essence of Woman, Updraft,* and *Fishmas*. She has edited multiple poetry anthologies, including *My Neighbor's Life*, *On Crimson Wings, Quilted Poems, Views of Virginia*, and *Blended Voices.* She delights in combining fiber art with the written word in anthologies like this one. Her website is www.KathleenDeckerAuthor.com

Zoey Dudding, freshman literary arts major at Appomattox Regional Governor's School for the Arts and Technology. In late winter of this year they won a gold key with Scholastic for fiction. They have been trying to master poetry. They live happily with six cats and one evil dog.

Dr. Jae Dyche's poetry has appeared in *Poet Lore, The Atlanta Review*, *Appalachian Review*, and *Hapur's Palette*. She earned her PhD in Rhetoric from Clemson University and her MFA in Poetry from the University of Maryland. Jae leads the Creative Writing program at Colgan High School's Center for the Fine and Performing Arts in Manassas.

Christie King Eckardt is a textile artist specializing in medium to large-scale art quilts using commercial and hand-dyed fabrics. Inspired by the natural and supernatural world often missed in our digital world, she uses raw-edge, fusible appliqué techniques to create intricate, unusual pieces that ask the viewer to pause and engage. Her award-winning quilts have been exhibited internationally and appeared in print.

ARTIST/POET/SCIENTIST BIOS, cont'd.:

Kerry Faraone is a fiber artist who has been creating and showing around the country for close to two decades. Her works have been published in over 16 books and has several pieces in private collections. Kerry transplanted with her husband and 4 children around 35 years ago from NY to Purcellville, Va., where they happily reside in the Loudoun countryside...enjoying the natural world around them.

Dr. Catalina Florina Florescu was born on a Sunday immediately after International Women's Day. She grew up close to the Danube River and has been accompanied by water her entire life. She started to write and publish after she earned her PhD in the States. While she found a lot of joy conducting academic research, the style became increasingly overwhelming; so, she has dedicated her last decade or so to writing poetry, plays, short fiction, etc. In part, she credits the switch to reading countless children's stories when her son was young. In part, she credits her investment in creative writing to being closer to her childhood water. Everything flows and evolves. Her books are catalogued at the Library of Congress, Princeton, Harvard, and other universities. http://www.catalinaflorescu.com/

Anna Isabella Fratarcangelo is a senior Literary Arts major at the Appomattox Regional Governor's School. She has received six Silver Keys and two Gold Keys in poetry from the Scholastic Art & Writing Awards; placed 2nd in the 2022-2023 VHSL Nonfiction Contest; a 2022 -23 National Youth Correspondent; 2nd in a 2023-2024 Poetry Society of Virginia memorial contest; and finalist in the 9[t]h Annual Narrative Magazine High School Writing Contest.

Chapman Hood Frazier's *The Lost Books of the Bestiary was* published in 2023 by V Press LC. His work has appeared in *The Virginia Quarterly Review*, *The Southern Poetry Review* and has won numerous awards. Currently a Professor Emeritus from James Madison University, he lives in Rice, Virginia and is co-managing Bellfield Farm LLC, a writer's retreat.

Dr. Dennis Owen Frohlich is a professor of media and journalism at Commonwealth University of Pennsylvania. Poetry is one of many creative outlets he pursues to keep his heart, mind, and spirit fresh. His poems have been published in the *Asahi Haikuist Network, Akitsu Quarterly, Altered Reality Magazine, the Bamboo Hut, Consilience, Failed Haiku*, and *Poets for Science*, among others. See more at http://dennisfrohlich.com/

Gail Giewont chairs the Literary Arts department at Appomattox Regional Governor's School for the Arts and Technology. Her chapbook of poetry, *Vulture*, is available from Finishing Line Press. She has won the Shann Palmer Poetry Prize, the *Many Mountains Moving* Poetry Prize, and the Fralin Museum's Writer's Eye Poetry Prize, among others. She lives in North Chesterfield, Virginia, with her rescue beagles, Bob Barker and Bee.

Dr. Michale Glennon is a Senior Research Scientist at the Paul Smith's College Adirondack Watershed Institute. She is an ecologist and uses wildlife as a tool for understanding threats to ecological integrity and watershed health. Michale also leads Wool and Water. This collaborative data art project uses knitting, crochet, and other fiber arts to tell the stories of the waters in the Adirondacks and beyond.

ARTIST/POET/SCIENTIST BIOS, cont'd.:

Marjorie Gowdy writes and paints on a farm in the Blue Ridge Mountains. She is the retired founding director of the Ohr-O'Keefe Museum of Art in Biloxi, MS, and a former grants writer in medicine and the arts. Author of three poetry chapbooks, Marjorie is inspired by lush, rolling landscapes which open as a book full of tales both exquisite and bittersweet. Her latest chapbook, *Pillow Fight*, (Prolific Press, July, 2024)

Jody Gruendel was born and raised in Northern Virginia. She has always had a love of art whether it be painting, fiber art, or art appreciation. Jody is a long-time quilter who currently focuses on art quilts. She enjoys the freedom of creating without a pattern to see where her vision takes her. Jody is a member of Studio Art Quilters Associates (SAQA) and her local Williamsburg, Virginia Art Tribe art quilters group.

Dr. Laura Guertin is a Distinguished Professor of Earth Sciences at Penn State Brandywine (Pennsylvania, USA). Trained as a marine geologist, she has a passion for engaging in innovative educational and outreach activities to improve the science literacy of all individuals of all ages. She uses quilts as one of her science storytelling communication tools to connect with audiences and share her field experiences on the coast and on ships at sea.

Cathy Hailey teaches in Johns Hopkins University's online MA in Teaching Writing program. She served as Northern Region Vice President of The Poetry Society of Virginia for 6 years, co-hosts Virginia Voices, and organizes In the Company of Laureates. Her chapbook, *I'd Rather Be a Hyacinth*, was published by Finishing Line Press. Recent publications include *Little Free Lit Mag, First Frost,* and *FotoSpecchio.* Visit cathyhailey.com.

Lauren Haygood is a Ph.D. candidate in the Boone Pickens School of Geology, Oklahoma State University. She earned her B.Sc. and M.Sc. in Geosciences from The University of Tulsa. She is interested in biogeochemical, hydrogeochemical, and geospatial analyses of aquatic environments. She is actively involved in geoscience education, outreach, science policy, and science communication. She enjoys problem solving and learning new techniques.

Kate Hedstrom was taught sewing, knitting and crochet by her mom when she was young. She has since learned other fiber arts, notably embroidery via online classes during the pandemic. Her science involves computer modeling of the oceans and sea ice, so she turns to colleagues for more inspiring images. Kate is active in the local spinning and weaving guild and can also be found on Ravelry.

Wayne David Hubbard is an award-winning poet, a Pushcart Prize nominee, and author of *Death Throes of the Broken Clockwork Universe*. He is the Treasurer of the Poetry Society of Virginia with works featured in various journals on the topics of science and human experience. Born and raised near Newark, New Jersey, he lives in the Shenandoah Valley and works in air traffic control. waynedavidhubbard.com .

Mark Hudson won second place in the 2025 "Dr. Lucile E. Thompson: Celebrating Women in Science and Technology" category in the Poetry Society of Virginia Annual Contest, and has several pieces accepted for the "Making the Unseen Seen" ekphrastic anthology. The irony? Growing up, science was one of Mark Hudson's worst topics! Mark Hudson likes to learn new things through writing poetry. He likes to spend time at the library!

ARTIST/POET/SCIENTIST BIOS, cont'd.:

Piper Jameson is currently a sophomore at Appomattox Regional Governor's School. She loves poetry and fiction, and aside from writing, she enjoys singing, playing sports, baking, and hanging out with friends. She is excited to have her poetry to be published, and thanks her poetry teacher, Gail Giewont, for helping her writing grow.

R. J. Keeler was born in St. Paul, Minnesota, and grew up in the jungles of Colombia. He holds a BS in Mathematics from North Carolina State University, an MS in Computer Science from the University of North Carolina-Chapel Hill, an MBA from the University of California at Los Angeles, and a Certificate in Poetry from the University of Washington. An Honorman in the U.S. Naval Submarine School, he was Submarine Service (SS) qualified. He is a recipient of the Vietnam Service Medal, Honorable Discharge, and a Whiting Foundation Experimental Grant. He is a member of IEEE, AAAS, and the Academy of American Poets. He is a former Boeing engineer. His first poetry collection, *Detonation*, and his second collection, *Snowman*, were published in 2020. His third collection, *The Open Gate*, was published in 2021. His fourth collection, *The Oil Fields of Tibú*, is searching for a publisher.

Dr. Carolyn Kreiter-Foronda is a Poet Laureate of Virginia, (2006-2008). She has co-edited three anthologies, co-authored a poem-play, and published nine books of poetry, including *The Embrace: Diego Rivera and Frida Kahlo*, winner of the international Art in Literature: The Mary Lynn Kotz Award. She is the recipient of five grants from the Virginia Commission for the Arts and won the Ellen Anderson Award, a Virginia Cultural Laureate Award, multiple first place awards from the Chesapeake Bay Branch of the National League of American Pen Women, a resolution of appreciation from the Virginia Board of Education for service as Poet Laureate, an Edgar Allan Poe Poetry Award, six Pushcart Prize nominations, as well as other awards. Her poems are featured in permanent art installations in Northern Virginia, along with other Poet Laureates, as part of the Washington Metropolitan Area Authority, Art in Transit installation.

Barbara Martina Linde spent a creative childhood learning hand embroidery from her grandmother and dressmaking from her mother. She started making up stories as soon as she could talk, and began writing her own stories at an early age. Her professional work as a reading specialist segued into a second career as a writer/editor of educational materials, including writing >150 books for children. Barbara began quilting in 1976, and now focuses on hand or machine applique and bead work. She combines her interests by writing poems to accompany her fabric creations. Barbara lives in Yorktown, Virginia with her husband and a large fabric/bead/thread stash.

Sally Harcum Maxwell After years of managing a successful medical practice, she needed to find her own voice. Art quilts are her chosen medium for self-expression because of her family heritage and the freedom to work with many techniques. She loves the feel of fabric!

Greg McNamara is an Australian geologist and geoscience educator with specialist interests in sedimentology and vertebrate palaeontology. His interest in science is eclectic and he enjoys teaching science at all levels.

ARTIST/POET/SCIENTIST BIOS, cont'd.:

Susan Copley Novack taught special education in middle school for 25 years in Fairfax County, Virginia. She did team teaching in eighth grade physical science classes where the students learned about solar and lunar eclipses, as well as the orbits of the moon and earth. She began quilting around 1982 and finds you can get more quilts completed once you retire.

Holly Panzera was born and raised in upstate New York. She attended New York School of Interior Design. She changed course and pursued a 35-year career in Nursing and Legal Consulting and now has returned to her original passion which is self-expression through fiber art. She is drawn to fiber art in all forms, including hand-dying and embellishing natural fiber. She began quilting traditional quilts and then discovered the freedom and creativity of art quilts. Holly enjoys researching symbolism used in painting and incorporating those symbols into her wall art. She currently lives in Williamsburg, Virginia.

Sarah Parker is a retired application and product development manager from a major instrumentation company. Explaining technical concepts and applying new technology to challenging applications were common tasks. Her environmental interests reach far back in her career development and her sewing interests even further. Upon retirement, combining the two areas became possible with art quilts. Using quilts to illustrate concepts is a natural fit.

Tessa Peixoto is a marine science professional and science communicator that has worked across the many fields of education, research, and business development. She has always enjoyed the opportunity to be creative and had a bout of intense poetry writing when she was younger. Now as an adult, her creativity comes in the form of finding innovative solutions to issues that arise in a project or differentiating lesson plans to be engaging and fun. She finds the best artistic overlap in the field of science communication where she is flexing her poetry muscle a bit more as she writes social media posts, blogs, and produces graphic designs for scientific research. Her main goal is to build a science-literate society that does not have to love the sciences, but does not fear it either.

Suzanne Underwood Rhodes is the Arkansas Poet Laureate and author of six poetry collections, including *The Perfume of Pain* and the award-winning *Flying Yellow.* Her poems appeared recently in *Southern Voices: 50 Contemporary Poets, Dappled Things, Spiritus,* and other publications. She teaches virtual poetry workshops through the Muse Writers Center in Norfolk, Virginia, and brings "Poetry on Purpose" to residents in a local memory care center. She is Arkansas's Individual Artist of the Year 2025.

Lynne Schreiber works as a project manager at the San Diego Supercomputer Center and lives in Sarasota, Florida. She loves touching things and working with her hands. Naturally, she gravitated to both pottery and sewing. It did not take long for her to realize that she will never run out of new ideas to try, problems to solve or colors to coordinate. Over time, these art forms have become a pathway for creativity, community, and lifelong learning.

ARTIST/POET/SCIENTIST BIOS, cont'd.:

Dr. Mattie Quesenberry Smith instructs Writing and Rhetoric I & II at Virginia Military Institute. In 2024, she earned her Ph.D. in curriculum and instruction from Virginia Tech. She studies critical reflective writing within technology and engineering design thinking. Raised in Appalachia, her poetry explores the natural world where poetic expression and scientific reason collide. She is the Virginia Poet Laureate (2024-2026).

Ron Smith was the Virginia poet laureate from 2014 to 2016. He is the author of five poetry *Running Again in Hollywood Cemetery, Moon Road, Its Ghostly Workshop, The Humility of the Brutes,* and *That Beauty in the Trees*. Smith currently serves as Consultant in Poetry and Prose at St. Christopher's School and Poetry Editor at *Aethlon: The Journal of Sport Literature*. His poems have appeared in numerous periodicals and anthologies and have been translated into Spanish, Italian, and Japanese.

Alicia Swain is a feminist poet and author living in Richmond, VA. Her debut poetry collection, *Steel Slides and Yellow Walls*, releases in August of 2025 with Belle Isle Books. Her work appears in or is forthcoming in publications such as *The Vehicle, Half and One, Roanoke Review,* and *Vast Chasm.* She can be found on her website at https://aliciaswain.com/, on Bluesky as @aliciamswain.bsky.social, and on Instagram as @aliciamswain.

Betsy Wilkening is a learner, engineer, educator, environmentalist, volunteer, wife, mom and activist. Her career has spanned jobs in industry, preK-12 classroom teaching, teacher professional development, outreach education, and community engagement. She started *Stitch Your Science* with Dr. Laura Guertin in 2021. She loves knitting and quilting as a means of communicating important information to others. Betsy is a 5th generation Arizonan. Her ancestors first occupied lands of the Tohono O'Odham and Yaqui people in Tucson under the Mexican flag. Her Hispanic roots run deep in the Sonoran Desert. As her community is disproportionately affected by extreme heat, persistent drought and extreme storm events, she is passionate about empowering all to take action to build a more resilient community.

Diana Woodcock has authored seven poetry collections since earning her MFA in Creative Writing at the age of 52, most recently *Reverent Flora* (Shanti Arts, 2025), *Heaven Underfoot* (2022 Codhill Press Pauline Uchmanowicz Poetry Award), *Holy Sparks* (2020 Paraclete Press Poetry Award finalist) and *Facing Aridity* (2020 Prism Prize for Climate Literature finalist). A three-time Pushcart Prize nominee and Best of the Net nominee, she received the 2011 Vernice Quebodeaux Pathways Poetry Prize for Women for her debut collection, *Swaying on the Elephant's Shoulders*. Currently teaching at VCUarts Qatar, she holds a PhD in Creative Writing from Lancaster University, where she researched poetry's role in the search for an environmental ethic.

Nicole M. Zwolinski earned her BA in Creative Writing with a focus in poetry at St. Cloud State University (SCSU). She's had pieces published in *Firewords Quarterly, Flash Fiction Magazine, Feminine Collective*, and more. In 2024, Happy Tapir Press published her chapbook, *The minor inconveniences of infidelities. Dresses without pockets and other disappointments* was selected as a finalist in Quillkeepers Press 2025 Spring Chapbook Competition.

ARTIST/SCIENTIST STATEMENTS:

Sarah-Beth Bradley: "Vesper Shawl." This shawl was inspired by the wing shape of a bat - the scientific name for these diverse animals which are *Chiroptera*, meaning hand-wing. I used a soft brown gradient yarn to break away from the gothic stereotypes of bats and evoke a more nature-based feeling, more 'little brown bat' than one of the seven 'vampire bat' species that prey on sheep and cattle.

Emma Burkett: "The Seismic Shadow." We can't see inside our planet because it's too hot, too deep, and under incredible pressure. But when an earthquake (white star) occurs, two types of seismic waves are generated, P waves and S waves, that help us learn what's below the surface. P waves (pink) are like a scrunched slinky being pushed and pulled, they move straight by compressing and expanding. These waves can travel through both solids and liquids. S waves (blue), on the other hand, are like shaking a slinky up and down or side to side. They only travel through solids and can't move through liquids. When these waves hit the liquid outer core of Earth, P waves bend (or refract), changing direction, and S waves stop completely. This creates a "shadow zone," an area on Earth's surface where we can't detect direct seismic waves. By studying these shadow zones, scientists determined that Earth has a solid inner core and a liquid outer core. Even though we can't see it, seismic waves help map the deep structure of our planet!

Tricia Coulson: "Synapse." Life in its many unseen forms include the space between functioning nerve cells through which nerve impulses are transmitted and is called synapse. Aberrant synapse physiology may contribute to neurodevelopmental disorders such as Alzheimer's disease. The synapse has consistently been considered a vulnerable and critical target within Alzheimer's disease, and synapse loss is one of the main biological correlates of cognitive decline. Several microscopic images of nerves and cord like fibers make up this piece. The addition of sequins add a sparkle of light to simulate the electrical impulses. Appliqued and embellished with sequins.

Marcela Bianchessi da Cunha-Santino: "Microorganisms in action, a microscopic view of leaf decomposition." This textile creation aims to microscopically show the microorganisms that act in the decomposition of lignocellulosic fibers in leaves with a magnification of 10,000 times.

Dr. Kathleen P. Decker: "The Unseen Battle." This quilt was created by printing electron micrographic photos of SARS-CoV-2 neutralizing antibodies onto fabric (Photo credit Dr. Christopher Barnes, Caltech, 2020), then stitched using raw edge appliqué, and embellished with Angelina fiber, metallic thread. Green beads highlight the active binding site to host protein Angiotensin Converting Enzyme 2 (ACE2).

Dr. Kathleen P. Decker: "Bioremediation." This fiber art piece was constructed using a plastic recyclable bottle cut in half, stitched to the top of a quilt, along with smaller sections of the bottle. Embroidered chemical equations delineate the stages of biodegradation of $[PET]_n$ (plastic) by *Idoenella Sakaiensis,* which secretes an enzyme that degrades PET using H_20, into MHET. *Idoenella* then takes up MHET and cleaves it to Ethylene Glycol (EG) and Terphalate (TPA). EG is fuel for other bacteria.

ARTIST/SCIENTIST STATEMENTS cont'd.:

Dr. Kathleen P. Decker: "The Amazing Endangered Ocean." Every species depicted on the right side of the art quilt is endangered. The quilt top was constructed by appliquéing layers, then creatures were embroidered on it. The left-hand side of the quilt depicts a kelp forest choked by invasive algae, and coral bleached and dying, with no sea creatures.

Christie King Eckardt: "Endoplasmic Reticulum." The labyrinth within the endoplasmic reticulum unfolds in a tapestry of structure and mystery, mirroring the complexity of life itself. Its precise, folded networks evoke a sense of mathematical order, yet the harmony of its form stirs something more intuitive- a quiet wonder. In this piece, I reflect on whether we, as humans, are shaped more by patterns of logic or by the pull of beauty, and if perhaps they are one and the same.

Kerry Faraone: "Sumatran Tiger." This is an Applique piece made with batiks from this area of the world. The animals of Sumatra are very important to me, mostly due to the loss of their territories to Palm Oil Harvesters...it is inhumane...I created a Sumatran Orangutan for the book "Inspired by Endangered Species " ..as I had contact as a child with Orangutans...and it still affects me. The chance to continue championing the animals of Sumatra is deep in me."

Kate Hedstrom: "Gelatinous Zooplankton." This work was inspired by the thesis defense of Hannah Kepner. She was studying the gelatinous zooplankton as seen by an ISIIS-DPI, an underwater imager taking shadowgraph pictures. It was also inspired by some embroidery classes I took online during the pandemic. Hannah's point is that we have vastly underestimated the number of these thing by sampling with net tows, the nets just destroying the soft tissue they are made up of."

Michale Glennon: "Recipe for a HAB ." This is a half-pi shawl depicting the conditions favorable for the formation of harmful algal blooms. A Harmful Algal Bloom, or HAB, is a phenomenon that occurs when colonies of algae grow out of control, occasionally producing toxins that can kill fish, mammals, and birds and cause human illness. HABs are a growing problem in waterways everywhere. This shawl depicts the conditions favorable for the formation of harmful algal blooms which include sun, warm, calm water, and nutrients. In this improvised shawl the sun is at the top and solid color rows depict warming water temperature. Next is a section of wavy stitches followed by plain garter stitch which depicts the transition to calm conditions. Beads represent nutrient inputs. At the bottom edge, the combination of these factors – sun + warm, calm conditions + nutrients – results in HABs represented by bright green roving. Though HABs themselves are often highly visible, this piece attempts to visually represent the conditions that often lead to HABs and therefore increase our knowledge and ability to predict these events. Part of Wool and Water, a collaborative data art project of the Paul Smith's College Adirondack Watershed Institute which uses fiber art to illustrate issues affecting our waters in the Adirondack Park and Lake Champlain Basin (adkwatershed.org/wool-water).

Michale Glennon: "Plankton." Plankton is an Irish crochet style wrap illustrating the issue of nutrient pollution in Lake Champlain and its impacts on plankton communities. Multicolored yarn motifs are meant to represent a variety of zooplankton, and the blue-green are meant to

ARTIST/SCIENTIST STATEMENTS cont'd.:

Michale Glennon: "Plankton," cont'd.:

represent blue-green algae (cyanobacteria). Moving from one end to the other, the blue green are increasingly represented while the multicolored (zooplankton) are reduced, indicating an observed plankton community shift. The basis for this piece is a study by Bockwoldt et al. (2017) which found reduced phytoplankton and zooplankton diversity associated with increased cyanobacteria in Lake Champlain. The cyanobacteria increase is attributed to increased nutrient input including phosphorus which can contribute to harmful algal blooms. Both the plankton themselves and the underlying nutrient loading are generally unseen. Part of a Wool and Water, a collaborative data art project of the Paul Smith's College Adirondack Watershed Institute which uses fiber art to illustrate issues affecting our waters in the Adirondack Park and Lake Champlain Basin, adkwatershed.org/wool-water.

Marjorie Gowdy: "The Variegated Fritillary." I live on a 100-acre farm that follows a stream north to south beside the eastern edge of the Blue Ridge Mountains. This route seems to be popular with birds and butterflies. The variegated fritillary is one of the most active butterflies on our farm at midsummer, particularly enjoying the Black-eyed Susans and Coneflowers. This is a pencil sketch later filled in with watercolor.

Marjorie Gowdy: "The Tortoise is Here." This young box turtle was meandering along the side of our country road last spring, but did allow me to move him into higher grass. Before I moved him (or was it her?), however, I took a photo. At home, I made this mixed media, non-representational play on the beautiful colors of a tortoise shell. Nothing really can surpass the glory of nature, but I enjoyed using acrylics, pencil, and beads to come up with "The Tortoise is Here."

Jody Gruendel: "Frosty Snowfall." It was initially inspired by a frosted, leaded glass window in the bathroom of a Front Royal, Virginia B&B where I was staying. I was intrigued with the pretty design letting in the filtered daylight yet giving privacy. Eventually, I found these fabrics offering the soft, muted tones reminiscent of a snowy day and the peaceful quiet of snowflakes accumulating outside. Who doesn't love to watch snow falling from a cozy indoor view?

Dr. Laura Guertin "DPS Got to Go Round." This quilt calls attention to the importance of the Dynamic Positioning System (DPS) of JOIDES Resolution, a scientific drilling vessel that collected deep sea sediment and rock cores during two-month research expeditions in all ocean basins across the globe. Dynamic positioning allows vessels at sea to remain in a geographic position without an anchor through utilization of thrusters and propellers. I sailed on this ship in 2022 for IODP Expedition 390 (South Atlantic Transect 1) and never saw the DPS components, as they were under the hull of the ship and under water. However, the DPS was essential in allowing us to accomplish our scientific objectives, as without this system, we would never have been able to successfully collect the deep sea material. JOIDES Resolution relied on its six thruster pods and two ship propellers to hold its position during deep-sea drilling activities. Although there are several additional inputs necessary for the Dynamic Positioning System to fully function (wind speed/current, GPS position, data from the motion reference units (MRUs), the

ARTIST/SCIENTIST STATEMENTS cont'd.:

Dr. Laura Guertin "DPS Got to Go Round," cont'd.:

orientation of the two ship rudders, etc.), this quilt pays tribute to those DPS parts that "go 'round". The yellow/gold colors represent the brass alloy of which the propellers are composed. The thruster blades are paired to represent the thruster pods as they exist on the ship, and they are stitched on to red fabric to represent the color of the ship's hull. The red fabric for the hull is a Da Gama Textile (Three Cats Shweshwe) manufactured in South Africa, where the ship departed from/returned to for my time at sea during Expedition 390. The blue spiral metallic fabric represents the motion of the water when the thrusters rotate.

Dr. Laura Guertin: "TAKK, *JOIDES Resolution* ." In September 2024, the International Ocean Discovery Program concluded. At that time, the scientific drilling vessel JOIDES Resolution (JR) concluded its participation across three international marine research collaborations - Ocean Drilling Program (ODP, 1983-2003), Integrated Ocean Drilling Program (IODP, 2003-2013), and the International Ocean Discovery Program (IODP, 2013-2024). In addition to the 194 expeditions and the >360,000 meters of core recovered during JR's time at sea, numerous significant scientific discoveries have been made and will continue to be made from archived core material that advance our knowledge of Earth's history, processes, and structure. These discoveries and more would not be possible without the dedication and tireless efforts of the technicians and crew that have worked aboard JOIDES Resolution. Without their time and expertise, these scientific advancements would remain mysteries in the deep sea. At the end of May 2024, a meeting of the IODP Expedition 390 & 393 onboard and onshore scientists, as well as students and mentors that are continuing investigations on recovered material, was held in Reykjavík, Iceland. Reflecting upon that moment in time, when JOIDES Resolution was about to set off on its final IODP expedition from Amsterdam, those gathered for the Post-Expedition science meeting took a moment to express appreciation to the ship and those that have worked to provide the material and measurements. This quilt captures those thoughts in the form of thank-you notes, appearing as if they are on the inside of an envelope. The envelope fabric is a Da Gama Textile called Three Cats Shweshwe, manufactured in South Africa. Both IODP Expeditions 390 and 393 departed from and returned to Cape Town, South Africa. The use of this fabric was intentional as a connection back to where JR was in port before, after, and in-between these expeditions. ("Takk" means "thank you" in Icelandic).

Lauren Haygood: "A Bag of Geoscience." "This is a bag that I crocheted. It has lots of pockets and an inside lining that is fabric material. There are lots of sections that are supposed to represent core material that can be recovered (e.g., ice cores and sediment cores), as well as a small ship representing the JR and scientific ocean drilling. The colorful yarn used on the bag identifies all the different (geo)science disciplines that come together to carry out collaborative international research. The lining represents the ocean. There are pieces of material incorporated in the bag from expeditions I have been involved with. The bag is bordered with sparkly yarn, which signifies the exciting (geo)science research and results that come from these collaborative research expeditions."

ARTIST/SCIENTIST STATEMENTS cont'd.:

Lauren Haygood: "Searching for Earth's Secrets: Hidden Impacts of Deep-Sea Sediments." Ocean basins are unique, and are connected via thermohaline circulation. Deep-sea sediment cores recovered during scientific ocean drilling expeditions contain clues about Earth's past. Although these clues are typically hidden within the sediments, geoscientists of all disciplines can apply multiple analyses and methods to extract these clues of Earth's past from deep-sea sediments. Within this crochet project, there are multiple different yarns, yarn colors, crochet stitches, and fabric used to create a large piece showcasing the hidden impact of the information preserved in deep-sea sediments.

Mark Hudson: "Crocodile." I Googled images of crocodiles, then used a pen and colored pencil to create the crocodile. This artwork represents my best artwork because it uses color.

Mark Hudson: "Seagulls Dumpster Diving." This drawing shows seagulls eating junk food on the dumpster which I felt matches the poem. I chose this to be black and white because seagulls are white, so a color picture wouldn't make sense.

Mark Hudson: "Toxic River Denizens." I tried to find a picture of the Pied Piper, but didn't find one. So, I settled for drawing a fish and a rat, which matches the spirit of the poem well.

Barbara M. Linde "Solar Eclipse Glasses." The wall hanging is made with the Rustic Mountain Snowflake paper piecing pattern from www.allpeoplequilt.com. I added glasses to demonstrate how to view solar phenomena during the eclipse safely.

Sally Harcum Maxwell: "Cedar Spirits." "Quarantine," "stay-at-home orders"—meant staying in a town named Poquoson. Also spelled *pocosin*, the name means *great marsh* and it made me think of the marshes and the Native Americans who populated this area before English settlers. I was reminded of a Cherokee creation story*. The People have realized mistakes and asked the Great Creator to divide time into night and day. The lesson did not come without a cost and many people died. These deaths saddened the Great Creator, and their spirits were placed in the Cedar tree which grows in the marsh. My family has a tradition to cut a cedar tree from the marsh at Christmas. Could it be that my ancestors were honoring those Great Ancestors? Are we related in ways that we did not know? *http://bearmedicinewalker.com/2014/11/13/cherokee-legend-of-the-cedar-trees-as-shared-by-bear-medicinewalker/

Sally Harcum Maxwell: "Family Farm." This is a small quilt that was made to honor my family farm heritage. It uses scraps of fabrics from family dresses to explain the layers of family attached to our land. It makes the footsteps and tire tracks visible, or "seen."

Sally Harcum Maxwell: "Roots VI." After the birth of my sixth grandchild, "family" was a topic on my mind. I was inspired by a quotation from Johann Wolfgang von Goethe: "There are two things parents should give their children: roots and wings. Roots to give them bearing and a sense of belonging but also wings to help free them from constraints and prejudices and give them other ways to travel." This quote made me think about the role of parents and the way they anchor their children and provide nourishment for their future growth. The quilt's background uses interconnected blocks called clamshells. Not only are they a reference to the clams that we harvest nearby, but also because they symbolize a closely connected family.

ARTIST/SCIENTIST STATEMENTS cont'd.:

Greg McNamara: "Colour in a Polarised World." Light is refracted as it passes from one material to another. In anisotropic minerals light refracts into two rays, each polarised at right angles to the other and travelling at different velocities. This is called birefringence. In petrological microscopy, polarised light is double-refracted through anisotropic minerals and polarised again. The resultant two rays interfere, producing interference colours. These colours enable mineral identification. In plain light rock thin-sections are mostly shades of rey and this colourful world remains unseen. Here, using the birefringence of layered sticky tape, the colours are metaphors for opinions refracted within the unseen realms of the mind. A circular faux-image of minerals (as might be seen through a petrological microscope) was created using the tape's birefringent properties. This image is reflected in the viewers eye, a small image with a big impact on the mind, just like ideas. The background hints at the range of possibilities, as seen in a Michel-Levy chart. The text about birefringence is set in a rhombic box with 'double writing' to echo the most extreme example of birefringence as seen in the rhombic mineral calcite· It speaks about a world of extreme opinions: the birefringence of calcite-like minds reduces conversation to a double refracted babble.

Susan Novack: "I Spy an Eclipse Safely." The sun's corona is usually obscured by the brilliance of the sun, unless special instruments are used. However, during a solar eclipse, the corona can be seen using eclipse glasses as a halo of bright light around the sun. This fiber art quilt shows solar glasses, with which it can be safely viewed during a total eclipse."

Holly Panzera: "'Ozone Depletion." communicates the story of volatile organic pollution and depletion of the ozone layer. The ozone layer, denoted by the chemical formula O3, is located in the stratosphere and surrounds the Earth. Volatile organic compounds (VOC), hydrochlorofluorocarbons (HCFC), and chlorofluorocarbons (CFC) deplete the ozone layer. This allows an increase in UVB rays reaching the Earth's surface. UVB rays play a major role in the development of cataracts and skin cancers. My hope is the combination of science and creative fiber art will encourage awareness, conversation and solutions.

Sarah Parker: "Climate Changes are Subtle but Fast." These quilts are a visual representation of daily high and low temperatures in Minneapolis over the course of a year. One quilt represents a 5 year daily average of high and low temperatures between 1978-1982 and the other quilt represents the same information between 2016-2020.

Sarah Parker: "In Minnesota, the Winters are Getting Warmer and Wetter." The amount and characteristics of snowpack that is on the ground changes throughout the winter. At one time, the snow cover was consistent all winter. There will be snow, but then it melts and there is bare ground. Instead of a fluffy dry snowfall, there is more freezing rain and icy precipitation. The snowpack comes and goes. If snow does stay, it becomes harder and icier. Some trees need colder weather to thrive. Many of our northern conifers are dying out and being replaced by hardwoods that previously grew further south. Great gray owls hunt for prey under the snow cover. They drop down into the soft fluffy snow to get the rodents. IF the snow is icier, they can't break through to get their prey. They leave and go further north. Moose are more

ARTIST/SCIENTIST STATEMENTS cont'd.:

Sarah Parker: "In Minnesota, the Winters are Getting Warmer and Wetter.," cont'd:

susceptible to ticks that thrive in the warmer weather, sickening the moose. Also, moose and snowshoe hare compete for the same food supply which is at different due to the lack of snow. Snowshoe hares are also declining due to lack of camouflage when the snow is not around making them more susceptible to the lynx and other predators. When snowshoe hare population declines, Canadian lynx population drops. Invasive species of plants and insects can survive the warmer winters. At one point, the cold temps would kill off new invaders. Now they can make it through the winter and live to damage trees. Warmer winters change habits of other creatures. Robins are more likely to stay around all winter. They are no longer the traditional harbinger of spring. Opossums are moving into areas where they were never seen before but are now common."

Lynne Schreiber: "Perspective." This work brings to life the perspectives in science that are often unseen. For a variety of reasons perspectives in science may not be seen: being discarded to the scrap bin; viewed as not necessary; lost in the bottom of a drawer; or imagined for another day when funding, resources or technology become available. With unseen perspectives in mind, this work was created from my 'discarded' and 'imagined for another day' fabric.

Seattle Asian Art Museum: "Monk at the Moment of Enlightenment." A Buddhist monk at the moment of enlightenment, when the spirit succeeds in breaking through the constraining barrier of human ignorance. This image likely represents a Buddhist monk at the moment of enlightenment, when the spirit succeeds in breaking through the constraining barrier of human ignorance. It is a moment of intense mental struggle and often associated with actual physical pain. The monk's figure is wonderfully dynamic, with a strong twist in the torso and a distinct tension between the two limbs, one thrusting forward, the other pulling back. The legs are crossed but hardly static, pointing in opposite directions. The visual sense of movement is further emphasized by the monk's bold, flowing garments. – Article by Josh Yiu, 2011 Statue Date Ca. 14th Century Chinese, **Medium**: Wood with polychrome decorations. **Dimensions**: 41 x 30 x 22 in. (104.14 x 76.2 x 55.88 cm).

ARTIST/SCIENTIST STATEMENTS cont'd.:

Betsy Wilkening: "Heat Kills." Extreme heat kills more people than any other weather related event, yet it is often under reported. I chose a Sunburst pattern for my quilt using material for the sun's rays that are the same colors used to depict heat in weather maps. Each square represents different chapters in the extreme heat story. The 2023 deaths reported by medical examiners in Maricopa and Pima Counties in Arizona totaled 871. Tracking now includes data for Heat-Related, Heat-Caused and Heat-Contributed deaths. Undocumented Border Crossers succumb to the heat when forced to walk many miles. The square shows the border wall and a skull to remember Los Muertos. Others at risk include the unhoused, people with insufficient air conditioning, outdoor workers, the elderly and young, and drug users (especially meth users). Solutions include education and support for drug users (purple ribbon), providing adequate breaks for workers (clock), cooling centers, homeless shelters and housing (roof/heart symbols), water (bottle), and reaching out to check on your neighbors (phone icon). Lastly, shade is very important. The City of Tucson has committed to planting 10,000 native trees which can be sustained by stormwater in neighborhoods most in need. 2024 was another record-breaking year of heat in Arizona, and we must do more to protect those at risk and fight climate change."

INDEX	**PAGE(S)**

INDEX **PAGE(S)**

www.ingramcontent.com/pod-product-compliance
Lightning Source LLC
LaVergne TN
LVRC090254110826
845147LV00009B/738

9781962935838